teen's *guides*

LIVING
with
PEER PRESSURE
AND BULLYING

Also in the
Teen's Guides series

Living with Alcoholism and Drug Addiction

Living with Allergies

Living with Anxiety Disorders

Living with Asthma

Living with Cancer

Living with Depression

Living with Diabetes

Living with Eating Disorders

Living with Obesity

Living with Sexually Transmitted Diseases

teen's guides

LIVING
with
PEER PRESSURE
AND BULLYING

Thomas Paul Tarshis, M.D., M.P.H.

☑Checkmark Books®
An imprint of Infobase Publishing

Living with Peer Pressure and Bullying

Checkmark Books
An imprint of Facts On File, Inc.
132 West 31st Street
New York NY 10001

Library of Congress Cataloging-in-Publication Data

Tarshis, Thomas Paul.
  Living with peer pressure and bullying / by Thomas Paul Tarshis.
      p. cm.
  Includes bibliographical references and index.
  ISBN-13: 978-0-8160-7914-8 (hardcover : alk. paper)
  ISBN-10: 0-8160-7914-5 (hardcover : alk. paper)
  ISBN-13: 978-0-8160-7915-5 (pbk. : alk. paper)
  ISBN-10: 0-8160-7915-3 (pbk. : alk. paper) 1. Peer pressure in adolescence. 2. Peer pressure. 3. Bullying. 4. Adolescent psychology. I. Title.
  HQ799.2.P44T37 2010
  303.3'27—dc22
                                     2009024521

Checkmark Books are available at special discounts when purchased in bulk quantities for businesses, associations, institutions or sales promotions. Please call our Special Sales Department in New York at (212) 967-8800 or (800) 322-8755.

You can find Facts On File on the World Wide Web at http://www.factsonfile.com

Excerpts included herewith have been reprinted by permission of the copyright holders; the author has made every effort to contact copyright holders. The publishers will be glad to rectify, in future editions, any errors or omissions brought to their notice.

Text design by Annie O'Donnell
Composition by Hermitage Publishing Services
Cover printed by Art Print, Taylor, Pa.
Book printed and bound by Maple-Vail Book Manufacturing Group, York, Pa.
Date printed: April 2010
Printed in the United States of America

10 9 8 7 6 5 4 3 2 1

This book is printed on acid-free paper.

CONTENTS

■ ■ **1** What Is Peer Pressure?   1

■ ■ **2** When You Do Have a Choice:
Managing Sticky Situations   10

■ ■ **3** The Coercive Power of Peer Pressure   21

■ ■ **4** Who Are Your Friends, Really?   46

■ ■ **5** Are You Being Bullied?   58

■ ■ **6** The Risks and Rewards of Truth Telling   69

■ ■ **7** When Things Get Overwhelming:
Mental Health Problems   81

■ ■ **8** Taking Charge Yourself   101

■ ■ **9** Cyberbullying: The New Frontier   120

■ ■ **10** Being an Advocate: Helping Others Cope
with Bullying   128

■ ■ **11** Finding and Paying for Care   133

Glossary   139

Appendix: Helpful Organizations   142

Read More About It   156

Index   160

What Is Peer Pressure?

Paul was a high school freshman in a large public school. He had transferred to this school from a smaller private school, which he had attended from kindergarten to eighth grade. This transition was a major one. His grade school had been small, with only one classroom of eighth graders. Although Paul was shyer than some of his peers, being in the same school for many years helped him to develop friendships and made him feel comfortable. In addition, his mother was a well-liked teacher at the school, which gave him special status on campus.

Unfortunately for Paul, he had to face as a freshman a large public school full of strangers—not a single student from his private school had joined him. Paul worried about being able to make new friends. For the first few weeks of school, Paul kept to himself. His luck seemed to change when he was assigned a partner, Aaron, for a project in his English class. Paul happily took this opportunity to make a new friend. An added bonus was that the two were required to work outside of school together. That evening, when Paul told his mom about the positive turn of events, she was excited about the potential for social acceptance and flourishing friendships in store for Paul's future.

After school the next day, Paul went over to Aaron's house to work on their project. When Paul got to Aaron's house, he noticed that they were the only kids at home. Aaron said that his parents were divorced and that he lived with his dad, who worked the evening shift, so he had the house to himself every night. After sitting down at a table to begin work on their project, Aaron asked Paul if he had ever had beer before. Although he had not, Paul was very anxious to seem "cool" and "mature," so Paul replied that he, in fact, did have beer lots of times. At that answer, Aaron grinned and walked over to the refrigerator. He came back carrying about four bottles of beer, saying that there was "plenty more" where that came from. As Aaron extended his beer-laden hand in offering, Paul held his breath and reached out to grab the beer. Although Paul didn't have any real interest in drinking, and he was even less interested in getting in trouble with his family, he didn't want to lose a possible friendship. So Paul opened up his first can of beer, took a sip, and forced a smile.

PEER PRESSURE HAS MANY DIFFERENT FORMS

Peer pressure is present in everyone's lives in many different ways. Peer pressure is of particular importance for teenagers, because the choices made when dealing with peer pressure influence the success or failure of your future. As a teenager, you are at a critical stage in your life—forming your identity, choosing your friendships, and shaping your life as an adult. By the time you are a teenager, you have already been exposed to peer pressure in countless situations. The difference is that your parents or another caregiver have usually been close by to help guide your decision-making progress. Now, as a teenager, it is less likely that someone will be monitoring all the decisions you make, thus giving you more responsibility. In addition, as children get older, we know that friends and peer groups replace parents and become the biggest source of influence on behavior. As a teenager, the opinions of your friends and classmates are likely to be more important than the opinions of your parents. These include beliefs in areas such as clothes, school, music, and television shows as well as more serious topics including alcohol, drugs, and sexual activity.

Peer pressure may be defined as the influence of other people's perceptions on your decisions or actions. This may either be a group of people or even just one person. Peer pressure is not always a bad thing. For example, if you are in a particularly studious math class and your concern about what your peers will think if you do poorly on a test helps motivate you to challenge yourself and study harder, this will probably lead to a better grade on the test, feelings of accomplishment and pride, and a desire to continue putting extra effort into your schoolwork. In fact, the next time there is a test, you may find yourself putting more effort into preparation, not in response to what other people may think, but because you had many positive feelings from the first time you studied more and you now want to perform well for individual reasons. This is called positive peer pressure.

Negative peer pressure is different. Negative peer pressure occurs when you are influenced to do something that you know is wrong. There are many reasons why people give in to this pressure. Like Paul, it could be concern over losing a friend or making a new one. It could be concern about being teased, being left out of activities, or being bullied. You may feel that the consequences of *not* giving in to peer pressure are worse than feeling guilty about doing something that you know is wrong. As we will explore further in this book, the outcomes of giving in to negative peer pressure are almost always much worse than expected, and thus developing the skills to resist peer pressure is an important part of growing up.

Peer pressure comes in many forms. See which of the following you have experienced.

COMMENTS

A subtle form of peer pressure, comments can be made by classmates or peers outside of school. You may notice that some students are quick to criticize or make fun of people's hairstyles, weight, clothing, family, or dozens of other personal subjects. These comments are made so other people can hear them, trying to get laughter or point out their "flaws" as a person. They are usually made in a sarcastic manner. If you confront the person on their comments about you, they may say "I'm just trying to give you some advice," but in reality they are trying to pressure you to change something to be more like them. When people are being helpful and trying to give true advice, they will usually do it in a private conversation and in a nonjoking manner—which is how you can tell the difference.

MATERIAL ITEMS

Depending on where you live or the type of school you attend, there will be certain items that will be the most popular. Teens are usually exposed to both **direct** peer pressure—"Those shoes are horrible! You need to get something with style"—as well as **indirect** peer pressure, when it seems that everyone has the newest cell phone except you. Other items that tend to be affected by peer pressure include electronic items such as video games, iPods or other music players, clothes, shoes, and cars.

BEHAVIOR

Peer pressure to perform certain behaviors is the most important type of peer pressure to learn to resist. Behaviors that are subject

What's the Big Deal About Peer Pressure?

Negative peer pressure is at least partially responsible for each of the following:

- Smoking
- Teenage pregnancy
- Drug addiction
- Alcoholism
- Bullying
- School failure

to peer pressure include relatively minor issues, such as using the computer to chat when you are supposed to be sleeping, to more extreme behaviors, such as cutting class and sneaking out at night. Peer pressure is also arguably the biggest factor in determining whether teens begin to use cigarettes, alcohol, and drugs or engage in sexual behavior. Peer pressure can also influence teens to perform outright illegal acts with very serious consequences, such as robbery or assault.

PEER PRESSURE V. BEING BULLIED

When your behavior is influenced because of a real threat of harm ("If you don't steal that shirt I am going to beat you up!"), it is not peer pressure but rather bullying. Almost everyone is familiar with what it means to be bullied, and probably every teenager has experienced bullying (either personally or through witnessing acts of bullying). Bullying is different than peer pressure, and usually more extreme interventions are required to stop bullying. The most commonly accepted definition of bullying has three components. First, the bully has to do something with the intent to harm the victim. The harm can be physical (hitting, kicking, making direct threats, etc.) or emotional (spreading rumors, excluding the victim from activities, sending mean text messages). Second, there has to be an imbalance of power between the bully and the victim, with the bully having a higher level of power. Again, this can be either physically or through social standing (for example, being more popular at school). Finally, the acts intended to harm the victim must be repeated over time. It is when all of these criteria are met that someone is considered either a bully or a victim. However, even if you do not meet this "scientific" definition of bullying, even single acts of being victimized can have drastic consequences. There are some techniques that are similar for dealing with bullying and peer pressure. However, bullying often requires more intense interventions to stop.

RISK FACTORS FOR PEER PRESSURE

Regardless of who you are, most teens will face peer pressure on an almost daily basis, sometimes many times per day. Some teens are more likely to experience and give in to peer pressure, while other teens are better able to resist. There are many risk factors that may make you more likely to give in to peer pressure. Some of the most important risk factors are noted below.

RECENTLY MOVING OR CHANGING SCHOOLS

The older you are, the more difficult it becomes to change schools or move to a new city. Even teens who are outgoing and friendly experience increased levels of anxiety when faced with having to make new friends. In general, it is much easier to make friends in elementary school than in either middle school or high school. New students are often targets for peer pressure. This is because people know that new students are often in need of friends and may make a decision to do something they would not normally do in an attempt to fit in or make a good impression on their new classmates.

POOR SELF-ESTEEM AND CONFIDENCE

Probably the biggest risk factor for giving in to peer pressure is how you feel about yourself. Teens who lack confidence and are scared to make decisions on their own often have problems resisting peer pressure. When you lack confidence in making your own decisions, you are more likely to seek out the advice of others or follow along with what other students do in an effort to be accepted. When you have good self-esteem, you are less likely to care about what other people think, making you less susceptible to peer pressure.

LACK OF FRIENDS

Feeling like you don't have a group of friends that you can speak to or hang out with puts you at risk for peer pressure. This is also true if you have friends but do not feel close to them or are afraid that your friends may turn on you at any time. This is a big problem, because teens lacking friends are at risk for serious problems other than just peer pressure, such as depression, anxiety, and substance abuse. There are two ways in which a lack of friends affects your susceptibility to peer pressure. First, you may be concerned about trying to make new friends and thus want to go along with what other kids say to be accepted. Second, if you don't have friends to back you up, you are less likely to make a decision to go against your peers.

LACK OF HOBBIES OR INTERESTS
Students who do little more than attend school and then watch television or play video games as their main activities put themselves at risk for peer pressure. Having many activities in which you are interested is protective in many ways. To begin with, having extracurricular activities usually leads to new friends, as people with similar interests tend to choose the same pastimes. In addition, having a diverse set of interests that occupies your time makes you less likely to seek out new experiences that may be dangerous. Studies show that teens involved in activities such as sports do better in school, are less likely to use drugs, and have higher self-esteem and confidence.

POOR FAMILY SUPPORT
Teens who do not have a close relationship with their family members are at much higher risk to give in to peer pressure. Usually, this means having a close connection with your mother and father, but there may be other family members who can fill this void. Other examples of family members include older siblings (brothers or sisters), aunts, uncles, and grandparents. The most important feature of these relationships is communication—feeling free to ask for advice without fear of what your family will think about you. Teens who have these open lines of communication with their families are influenced less by peer pressure.

POOR SCHOOL PERFORMANCE
Doing poorly in school damages self-esteem and confidence and thereby increases your risks for giving in to peer pressure. Teens are usually aware of which of their classmates are not doing well and thus are less likely to be concerned about their overall behavior while at school. This in turn leads to an increase in being targeted by peers to do inappropriate behaviors that can lead to negative consequences.

What Is Hazing?

Hazing is a long-standing tradition of requiring new (or at times existing) members of a group to perform an act in order to join (or stay) in that group. Hazing is most often associated with college sororities and fraternities but actually extends across all areas of life. For teens, hazing is extremely common, especially with respect to making new friendships. Teenage hazing may consist of telling new kids that they must perform certain acts before they can "join" a new group. These acts could be humiliating for them, or they could require them to humiliate other students. Quite often, the hazing behavior that teens do does not give the results that the teens were expecting.

BEING AFRAID OF PEERS

If you are afraid of your peer group, either for safety reasons (you go to a school that has security guards due to repeated gang issues or drug use) or due to your own personality (being excessively shy or scared in social situations), you are more at risk for peer pressure.

BEING FRIENDS WITH BULLIES

Although it may seem like common sense, teens who are friends with the school bullies are more likely to participate in bullying behaviors themselves. Bullies are usually skilled at applying peer pressure and intimidation to their friends. It is important to examine your current friendships and decide if you are being pressured into bullying other students or feel that there is constant pressure to do activities that make you feel uncomfortable.

EMOTIONAL RESPONSE TO PEER PRESSURE

As children become teenagers, new emotions and feelings arise that begin to affect your thoughts and behavior. It is a commonly held belief that your thoughts, feelings, and overall mental health are connected. Below are some examples of how peer pressure situations can influence thoughts and feelings.

Situation	Sample Thought	Feelings
Several of your friends want you to cut class after lunch to go to the movies.	"I know I shouldn't go—if I get caught I will be in trouble."	*Nervous* about leaving school and getting caught.
You are offered a cigarette by some friends.	"I don't want my friends to call me a wimp for not trying one."	*Anxious* that you get picked on if you don't try one. *Scared* about doing something that is bad for your health and that you don't really want to do.
A friend of many years tells you he has been smoking pot many times a week.	"I can't believe my friend is smoking pot."	*Angry* that your friend is jeopardizing his health and school.
There is a party at a classmate's house whose parents are out of town. You know there will be alcohol there.	"That party will be fun, but I will have to lie to my parents and tell them adults will be there."	*Excited* about going to a party with your friends. *Concerned* that you will have to lie to your parents and that something bad may happen.
You told your boyfriend that you would have sex with him after dating for 6 months. It has now been over 5 months and your boyfriend keeps reminding you about what you said.	"I know I said that, but I don't feel ready." "I don't want him to break up with me."	*Curious* about doing sexual things for the first time. *Uneasy* about sexually transmitted diseases and getting pregnant.

Everyone has both positive and negative thoughts and feelings. As these thoughts and feelings occur, there is always an emotional response that is present as well. Depending on the situation, the response can be so intense that you have physical symptoms (body shaking, having a stomachache or headache, or feeling that your heart is beating super fast) that go along with your emotional response, which may include racing thoughts, feeling that you can't sit still, or crying. During the first few years after puberty, emotional responses tend to be more extreme and then decrease as you get older. Because of this fact, teens who are repeatedly subjected to peer pressure without having strategies to deal with it often find themselves feeling trapped in cycles of negative thoughts and feelings. When these thoughts and feelings are maintained for more than a few hours or few days, they can lead to more serious problems such as major depression or an anxiety disorder.

WHAT YOU NEED TO KNOW

- Peer pressure is when you feel the need to change how you act to feel accepted by another individual or group.
- There are different forms of peer pressure—both positive and negative. Positive peer pressure can help push you to succeed, but negative peer pressure can influence you to do things that have bad consequences.
- Peer pressure can be felt through comments others make, pressure to buy material items, or pressure to behave in a certain way or engage in a certain activity.
- Bullying is different from peer pressure because there is a direct threat of physical or emotional harm for not doing something, and it is repeated over time by the same person.
- There are many risk factors for peer pressure. Some of the more common ones include poor self-confidence, lack of self-esteem, poor relationships with friends or family, and poor school performance.
- There can be a wide range of thoughts and feelings associated with peer pressure that can influence your emotional state and possibly lead to feelings of depression and anxiety.

2 ▌▌▌

When You Do Have a Choice: Managing Sticky Situations

Molly was a 14-year-old girl who had moved to a new school for freshman year. Fortunately for Molly, being an outgoing and social person enabled her to join a group of girls soon after starting at her new school. Her social calendar both at and outside of school was now filled with color guard practices, trips to the mall, and birthday parties. Molly couldn't have been happier for finding a fun and accepting group of friends.

One day, when hanging out with her friends on a Friday afternoon, one of them pulled a joint out of her purse. They were all giggling excitedly and started to pass around the lit joint. As she saw the joint make its way around the circle of girls, Molly knew that she had to act quickly. The thing was that Molly had made up her mind a long time ago that she was not interested in using drugs. She had learned about the potentially ruinous effects of drugs on everything—school, activities, and friendships—but at the same time, she was so happy about having new friends that she was worried that not participating in the activity would render her an outcast. Thinking swiftly, Molly told her friends that she had to get ready for gymnastics practice (all of her friends knew that she took gymnastics lessons in addition to her participation in color guard) and had to leave. All the girls looked up at her from their tight little circle and acknowledged her leaving. Some of them had begun to look like they were getting high already.

Molly realized that her current group of friends was participating in behavior that was inappropriate. For Molly, doing well in school and in her extracurricular activities, such as color guard and gymnastics, was important. She did not want to jeopardize her performance with drugs, but at the same time, she was very social and keenly wanted to feel socially accepted. What would she do? She began to see a potential new social outlet in the members of her gymnastics class. Even as her friendships with the gymnastics girls strengthened, Molly remained on good terms with her initial group of friends. However, Molly learned to create boundaries with the initial group of friends. She still cherished the memories they had made in the beginning and was grateful for their acceptance, but she restricted her time with them to include only times when she knew drugs wouldn't come into the equation. Ultimately, she created her own identity and social network with a fine balance between both circles.

STICKY SITUATIONS ARE INEVITABLE

No matter what, you are going to face situations in which you will have to make a choice: Do you give in to peer pressure, or do you make a decision that you will feel better about, regardless of what others think? For each teen, some situations will be easier to manage than others. Your ability to handle "sticky situations" is based on many contributing factors. Some of the most important ones include:

- Self-esteem—How well do you like yourself, and do you feel confident and satisfied with your behavior?
- Morality—What are your personal beliefs regarding right versus wrong? These beliefs are shaped by influences such as parents, religion, peers, and other societal influences.
- Friends—How strong are your friendships, and how many friends do you have?
- Family—Do you have good support from your family? Are you able to communicate clearly with your parents or other family members without fear of what they will say or do to you?

Even though there is no way to prevent all the situations in which you will experience peer pressure, there are steps you can take to increase your awareness of your surroundings and anticipate when you may face a difficult situation. Most times, peer pressure happens at school or when you are spending time alone with your peers. When there are adults present, including teachers or family members, you are less likely to experience peer pressure. Read the situations that follow, and see how many times you have encountered similar circumstances.

THE NEW KID

You are sitting with your usual group of friends at lunch. A new student to the school that you met briefly in your second period class asks if he or she can sit with you. You thought the new student was nice, and you remember when you changed schools in fifth grade how hard it was to meet new friends. You are about to offer to let the new kid sit down when two of your friends at the table make faces at you, indicating that they don't want to let a new student join your group.

MAKING FUN

One of your classmates usually wears clothes that are hand-me-downs from her older sister. Even though they are hand-me-downs, they are not ripped or dirty. In your house, two of your younger siblings often get your old clothes and shoes that are still in good shape, and thus you understand why families do this to save money. Two of your friends who would "not be caught dead" in anything but new clothes begin to tease the student about her attire. The other student is clearly distressed by your friends' comments. You want to tell your friends to "shut up" but are worried about the effect this may have on your friendship.

CHEATING

You have been studying hard for your science test, which is your sixth period. At lunch one of your classmates shows a copy of the test from someone in the second period who snuck it out of the room. Several of your friends are figuring out the answers to the test ahead of time. They tell you to come help them. Even though you know your science grade could use a boost and would like to see the questions to the test, you are wary of doing something such as cheating that you know is wrong and may cause you to feel disappointed in yourself at a later time.

AT THE MALL

On the weekends, you and several of your friends usually meet at the mall to hang out and occasionally buy things. You notice that one of your friends suddenly has two new T-shirts. You ask her how she got them, and she tells you that she snuck them into a dressing room and put them on under her sweater. She says she knows there were no video cameras that saw her. Another one of your friends likes the idea and asks you to go back with her to steal some clothes.

GOING OUT

On Saturday you are invited to the movies. Normally, your parents give you a $10-allowance, but you got an advance this week because there was an item that you really wanted. Your parents warned you against taking an advance, saying that you usually need your allowance on the weekend when you hang out with your friends. To make a point, they decided not to loan you any money to go to the movies with your friend. You really want to meet up with your friends, but they are equally broke. They tell you, "Just grab 10 bucks out of your dad's wallet—he'll never miss it." You do know that your dad leaves his wallet unattended in his room when at the house and are pretty sure you could get away with taking some money.

THE SMART KID

All of your life you have been a good student. You spend a lot of time on your homework and study hard before tests. Because of this, you have a reputation as the class "brain." In elementary and middle school, you felt proud of this and of the respect you got from your teachers. You are surprised to find that things have changed in high school. Instead of receiving positive comments from your peers, they begin to make comments that you are a "teacher's pet" and a "nerd," and suddenly you don't feel like working as hard on your schoolwork, as you now feel that you are getting a negative reputation at school. You think about intentionally doing poorly in some of your classes to change your newly forming reputation.

LUNCH BREAK

Your school has an "open lunch" policy, in which you are allowed to go off campus during lunch. Usually you bring lunch from home or buy something at the snack bar from school, as most often you spend the lunch period in the library with two of your friends. One Friday a couple of the more popular kids at school are in your current events group in social studies and invite you to come off campus with them at lunch. Excited at the opportunity to develop possible friendships, you agree and meet them to head out to a nearby restaurant. While you are eating, your fellow students mention that they are not going back to class but rather are heading out to one of their homes to watch movies. They tell you to come with them and that they will help you by calling the attendance line, pretend that one of them is your mother, and tell the school you had a dentist appointment.

CHEW

It is common for you and your friends to get together after school or on weekends to play football. On this occasion, one of your friends brings along his brother who is two years older than the rest of you. You enjoy playing football all morning. At the end of the game, when everyone is talking, your friend's brother pulls out some chewing tobacco. He says, "All right guys, I'm in a sharing mood so everyone gather round for some chew." Your friends immediately huddle up to try some, leaving you lagging behind. You know that chewing tobacco is just as bad for you as smoking but feel nervous about what your friends will think of you if you don't try some.

DEPRESSED STUDENTS

You are psyched—it is the day of the museum excursion, and three of your good friends have been chosen to ride in the same car. Another student from your school, one of the "Emo" kids who is always depressed, is also coming in your vehicle. Your cousin has had problems with depression, so you have some understanding of what the other student is going through. When your friends see who the other student is, they rush over to you and tell you that they plan to ignore everything the other student says or does while in the car or at the museum and that you need to ignore him as well. You do not want to be mean to this other student but are worried what your friends will say if you stand up to them.

THE PARTY

As a high school freshman, you were excited to be invited to a party over the weekend hosted by seniors from your school. Since your parents have a rule that you are not allowed to attend unsupervised parties until you are older, you tell a "white lie," saying that you are going to sleep over at one of your friend's homes (who is also going to the party). You get a ride to the party with your friend's older brother, who, once you arrive, begins downing beers. Although you enjoy speaking with your friends at the party, you begin to feel nervous as it keeps getting later and you aren't sure how you and your friend will get back to her house. Finally, around 3:00 A.M., your friend wakes up her brother (who is still clearly drunk) and tells him to give you guys a ride back to their house. Her brother says OK, and you begin to make your way to his car. Although you know it is dangerous to get into the car with her brother, you are thinking about how angry your parents will be if they find out that you lied to them about going to a party.

THE "NEXT STEP"

You and your boyfriend have been together for four months. You told him when you started dating that you did not want to have sex until

Ethics Quiz:
Knowing Right from Wrong

There are two components to ethics that are relevant for teenagers. The first component is your ability to discern "right" from "wrong." The second is how well you follow through with either doing things that you feel are right or not doing things that you feel are wrong. Take the quiz below to get a better understanding of how you might handle peer pressure situations.

	Right thing to do?		Would you do it?	
1. Making fun of someone's clothes	YES	NO	YES	NO
2. Calling someone ugly or fat	YES	NO	YES	NO
3. Taking lunch from a peer	YES	NO	YES	NO
4. Throwing a book at a peer	YES	NO	YES	NO
5. Throwing a paperclip, spitball, or other small item at someone	YES	NO	YES	NO
6. Pushing someone	YES	NO	YES	NO
7. Slapping someone	YES	NO	YES	NO
8. Hitting or kicking someone with the intent to harm them	YES	NO	YES	NO
9. Texting mean comments	YES	NO	YES	NO
10. Threatening to hurt someone	YES	NO	YES	NO
11. Spreading rumors	YES	NO	YES	NO
12. Standing up for a friend who is being bullied	YES	NO	YES	NO
13. Alerting school personnel to threats toward a friend	YES	NO	YES	NO

(continues)

(continued)

	Right thing to do?		Would you do it?	
14. Alerting school personnel to threats toward a classmate you don't know	YES	NO	YES	NO
15. Standing up for a classmate you don't know who is being bullied	YES	NO	YES	NO
16. Teasing someone about a test score	YES	NO	YES	NO
17. Telling someone to intentionally harass another student	YES	NO	YES	NO
18. Telling a lie about someone to hurt one of his or her friendships	YES	NO	YES	NO
19. Reporting someone who is cheating on a test	YES	NO	YES	NO
20. Reporting someone who comes to school while intoxicated with drugs or alcohol	YES	NO	YES	NO

you were in college. At that time, he said that he understood and that he planned on waiting until he was much older as well. You enjoy the time you spend together and look forward to seeing him each day. One night while on a date, he tells you that he has been thinking about your relationship and feels that you are ready to "take the next step." He implies that if you will not agree to at least have oral sex, this will be the end of the relationship. Although you don't want to do any type of sexual activity, you don't want to lose your boyfriend, either.

PRACTICAL ADVICE TO MANAGE PEER PRESSURE

Although peer pressure is present in many situations and in many forms, your responses to handling peer pressure can often be applied to more than one situation. Having knowledge of several ways to deal with pressure and figuring out what strategies are helpful for you are a vital part of development. Whenever you are faced with peer pressure, learn to take a moment to reflect on the situation before acting. Below are some concepts for use in handling peer pressure.

PREVENTION IS THE BEST MEDICINE

In medicine, it is always easier to prevent an illness than to cure an illness. This is the concept behind such things as exercising, avoiding smoking, and eating healthy. The same concept can be applied to peer pressure. Knowing that there will be countless situations in which you will face peer pressure, assuming that such situations will occur, and being aware of your surroundings can minimize the number of times you are put "on the spot." Each morning, you should spend a couple of minutes thinking about your schedule for the day, noting times when you may be put in peer pressure situations. These may include days when there are changes to your regular schedule, such as field trips, after-school meetings, or parties. When you identify these times ahead of schedule, you will be more prepared to handle difficult situations when they arise. If you foresee severe circumstances, coming up with strategies ahead of time or changing your plans entirely may be the best options.

STRENGTH IN NUMBERS

If you have a group of friends you can rely on, you are already at less risk of experiencing peer pressure. We know from research that teens who have reliable friendships are less likely to worry about what their peers think and are more able to resist peer pressure. When you have a large group of friends, positive peer pressure can often replace negative peer pressure. For example, if someone in your group of friends is thinking of using drugs, you can rally the rest of your peers together to help them make the decision not to use, thereby creating a positive peer pressure situation. If you know you may be in a situation in which peer pressure will occur, take note of which of your friends will be with you and whether you can ask some of your friends to join you in resisting inappropriate actions.

WHO'S THE INSTIGATOR?

In most situations, there is usually one student who is responsible for instigating peer pressure. If you think about the people you know from your school or neighborhood, you may be able to identify which kids are the ones who always taunt others, make poor decisions, and try to get other teens to go along with them in their speech and actions. Keeping a mental list of which of your peers seem to always be in the middle of uncomfortable situations can help you be prepared for their comments and more easily resist peer pressure.

FIND AN ALLY

If you feel uncomfortable in a situation with your peers and think everyone else is OK with what is happening, you are almost certainly mistaken. As noted above, there are usually only one or two students trying to put pressure on others. Often, you may be able to identify an ally among the other people in your group. If you can find just one other student who also feels uncomfortable and can lend a voice in resisting the peer pressure, it can aid you in pushing back.

KEEP YOUR COOL

In all situations in life, being able to remain calm can help you think clearly and solve problems. Teens who are anxious are often easy targets in peer pressure situations. Those teens who are able to keep their cool, analyze the circumstances, and not show that they have any concerns will often immediately deflate the pressure from the situation. Being able to respond to peer pressure with calm, direct responses, such as, "For many reasons, I have decided not to drink any alcohol until I am older," can immediately end awkward moments.

HAVE BACKUP PLANS READY

Like Molly, thinking about ways to get yourself out of "sticky situations" before they occur can make you feel reassured about your ability to remain safe. Think about your life and try to identify different things you can say or do as a backup plan to avoid peer pressure. For Molly, knowing that she could excuse herself at a moment's notice for gymnastics gave her confidence in her ability to not engage in risky behaviors. Other backup plans may include:

> ➤ Having to meet a friend or family member
> ➤ Having to be sharp to prepare for a test or assignment
> ➤ Having to go to a doctor or dentist appointment

There are few people who would argue with you that you should engage in risky behavior when you have to meet up with your parents later in the day. Saying "If my mom or dad caught me doing that, it may be the last straw" will usually get other teens to lay off the peer pressure.

THINK ABOUT CONSEQUENCES

As children grow from elementary school, through middle school and high school, and then into adulthood, they get better at thinking about consequences to their actions. As a teen, you are still probably developing these skills. Some consequences are no longer an issue, such as running into the street without looking, which is a big concern for parents of small children. However, understanding the cost from other activities may not be so clear. For what may seem like a "minor" decision, such as having a beer at a party, there is always the possibility of a tragic result. Teasing other kids at school can lead to suicide and school shootings. Cutting class can lead to getting kicked out of school. Trying cigarettes, alcohol, or drugs can lead to more serious problems, such as addiction. Taking a moment to think about what may happen from giving in to peer pressure may provide you with valuable information to help you rethink your actions.

TRY HONESTY

When put in a "sticky situation," rather than acting honestly, your initial thoughts may be "How can I deal with this so I seem cool" or "How do I handle this without losing my friends" or "This would be a great way to change what people think of me." In peer pressure situations, there are many emotional signals that influence thought patterns. With practice, you can be aware of the emotional signals and change your reaction to peer pressure situations. This can allow you to think about the situation differently and respond in an honest manner about what is going on. Remaining calm and making comments such as "I understand why you are asking me to do that, but it is not something I feel comfortable with" can end these situations in a non-stressful manner.

FEEL GOOD ABOUT YOUR DECISIONS

As a teenager, you are going to make decisions that you feel good about and other decisions that may lead to negative consequences and feeling remorseful. Ultimately, you are the individual who will need to bear the consequences of your actions. The students who are encouraging you to make poor decisions are usually not going to feel remorseful if something bad happens to you. Thus, when faced with peer pressure situations, take a moment before responding. Think about the possible outcomes, and make a decision that you can feel good about. Making a bad choice can lead to many negative emotions, such as guilt, anger, stress, or remorse, and affect your mood, concentration, and ability to complete work. Making a decision you feel good about will not impair your concentration or mood and will probably improve your self-esteem.

LEARN FROM PAST EXPERIENCE

No one is perfect. It is unreasonable to expect teenagers or anyone else to resist peer pressure all the time. The biggest risk factor for giving in to peer pressure is how previous peer pressure situations have been handled. If you make a mistake and do something you regret, you should not spend time criticizing yourself. Instead, take it as a learning experience, and use it as a benefit to give you strength the next time you are in a similar situation. Keeping track of your feelings when dealing with the consequences (good or bad) from previous peer pressure situations provide the best clues for how to respond to similar situations in the future.

WHAT YOU NEED TO KNOW

- ▸ All teenagers will encounter "sticky situations" involving peer pressure.
- ▸ How we respond to "sticky situations" depends on many things, including self-esteem, our relationships with friends and family, and our sense of "right" and "wrong."
- ▸ "Sticky situations" can occur almost anywhere and often many times each day.
- ▸ Practicing how to handle "sticky situations" and planning your life to avoid them when possible can help manage peer pressure for teenagers.
- ▸ No matter what happens, if you can learn from peer pressure situations, it will make future situations easier to handle.

The Coercive Power of Peer Pressure

Jeff was a popular and well-liked sophomore in high school. Even though he was only a sophomore, he played on the varsity basketball team. He did well in school and had many friends. He was so popular, in fact, that he was often invited to hang out with older students and one Friday night found himself at an unsupervised party at a senior's house whose parents were out of town for the weekend. Jeff had an older sister who was a senior at the same high school. At the party, he recognized several people, including some members of the basketball team and his sister. He noticed that there was some passing around of beer bottles, hard liquor, and street drugs. Luckily, since Jeff had good self-esteem, he didn't feel the need to participate in the drug and alcohol use to impress his peers. However, Jeff knew that his sister did not have the same limits that he had with regard to alcohol. Occasionally, she did get drunk, and there was even a time last year when she was brought home by the police for public intoxication.

Midway through the party his sister had come up to him, begging him not to call his parents for a ride home, because she would lose her car if she was caught drinking again. Jeff told his sister that he wouldn't tell his parents. As the party was coming to an end, many of the students had already departed, and Jeff's sister was drunk. Jeff was worried because the party was many miles from his house and he didn't know how he and his sister were going to get home. They had gotten a ride to the party from one of his sister's friends, who was

21

also drunk. Now that it was time to leave, his sister got into the car with the friend that drove them over and told Jeff to get in. Jeff told his sister and her friend that he thought they shouldn't be driving. Several people still at the party heard this and told Jeff that he would be fine, that he shouldn't tell on his sister, and to stop being a loser. These teens still at the party said that if Jeff did something that got his peers in trouble, they would make it known around school that he was a "baby" and couldn't handle "real" parties. Flustered and feeling pressured, Jeff climbed into the back seat of his friend's car. He was not happy about the fact that he was in that car, but this time his responsible and caring traits were pushed to the side by his fear of being ridiculed by his peers.

PEER PRESSURE AND ALCOHOL

Teens may face more pressure to drink alcohol than any other activity. From an early age, children are exposed to alcohol through media such as television and movies and advertising via such things as billboards and magazines. Depending on the family, kids also develop views on alcohol based on what they see at home and at family gatherings. Often times, the use of alcohol is glamorized, such as in the media, or associated with positive feelings, such as family members enjoying alcoholic drinks on holidays, birthdays, and other occasions that kids remember fondly. Some teens may have differing views of alcohol use based on their families. Alcohol dependence (or alcoholism) is one of the most common and deadly substance addictions throughout the world. Given how common alcoholism is, it is unlikely that by the time you are a teenager you don't know someone who has a drinking problem. We know from research that if you have a family member (especially a parent, brother, or sister) who has a problem with alcohol use, you are at a much higher risk for becoming addicted to alcohol yourself.

The World Health Organization has ranked alcohol use as one of the biggest health concerns worldwide. Even if you are not an alcoholic, people who drink large quantities of alcohol only occasionally (which is the case for most teenagers and young adults) may have the same risks from drinking as chronic users of alcohol. Below are some of the issues associated with alcohol use:

HEALTH
Alcohol has negative effects on many organs and systems throughout your body.

Healing / immune system. Alcohol impairs how well your body can heal itself and also reduces your body's ability to fight off infection.

Bones. Alcohol use decreases the strength of your bones, which can lead to fractures and poor bone health as you get older.

Liver disease. Liver disease from alcohol use is a major cause of illness and death in the United States and throughout the world.

Obesity / nutrition. People who consume alcohol have poor dietary habits, leading to poor overall nutrition and a possible link to obesity.

Allergies. If you suffer from allergies, drinking even small amounts of alcohol can not only cause severe allergic reactions but can intensify your reaction to other allergens you may be sensitive to.

Cortisol. Cortisol is an important regulatory hormone in our bodies. It helps to regulate sleep, stress, memory and brain function, and even diabetes. Alcohol use causes disruption to the normal production and functioning of cortisol and can lead to the problems listed above.

Cancer. Alcohol use is associated with an increased risk for numerous types of cancer. These include lung cancer (probably by increased risk from smoking), breast cancer, colon cancer, head and neck cancer, bladder cancer, liver cancer, and others.

Tobacco. Alcohol use increases the risk that you will engage in the use of other drugs. Regarding tobacco, we know that people who drink the most alcohol are also people who smoke the most cigarettes. There is a large risk for teenagers from drinking alcohol, in that it can lead to trying cigarettes, which are highly addictive, and may lead to a smoking habit with dire health consequences.

SEXUAL ACTIVITY

Alcohol use is particularly relevant to sexual activity in teenagers. Teens usually have little control over knowing when to stop drinking, and this leads to perilous situations. Alcohol impairs communication and decision making. In addition, alcohol causes changes in emotions that often are already intense in teens. Combining these factors makes alcohol a risk factor for the following poor outcomes from sexual activity.

Pregnancy. Besides increasing the likelihood of sexual activity, alcohol impairs judgment, making it less likely that teens will be aware of the realities regarding becoming pregnant. Teens are less likely to use logical thinking (such as "I am too young to have sex" or "I want to wait until college before having intercourse") and especially unlikely to use birth control when engaging in sexual activity while drunk.

Rape. Alcohol use in teenage girls is associated with a much higher rate of rape and sexual assault than in girls who do not drink. Girls are more likely to put themselves in dangerous situations and feel pressured into sexual activity. Boys who drink may become more aggressive and be more likely to force sexual activity on their partners. Being drunk is not a valid excuse for criminal behavior, and the loss of judgment from alcohol can lead to lifelong consequences for teens who are guilty of sexual assault.

Sexually transmitted disease. As with pregnancy, impaired judgment may result in risky behavior without proper protection, leading to sexually transmitted diseases, some of which are incurable. More information about sexually transmitted diseases is listed later in this chapter.

DRUNK DRIVING

Almost every teenager has been informed about the risks of drunk driving since elementary school. There are national organizations dedicated to providing education and resources for teens and adults regarding drunk driving. As a rule, teenagers are new to driving and have limited experience behind the wheel. Adding alcohol to this equation leads to disastrous consequences. Alcohol impairs focus, judgment, concentration, and reflexes and can affect your vision and depth perception. Teens who are caught driving while intoxicated face a variety of legal consequences. If you are lucky, this may include the loss of your license and community service if you are pulled over for driving erratically. If you are in a crash or if you injure or kill someone, including passengers in your car, you may spend years in jail—all from making the one mistake to use alcohol and then drive.

Drinking alcohol also leads to an increase in accidents and death for teens when not driving. Walkers, bike riders, and skateboarders who are intoxicated are more likely to be injured or killed if performing these activities while intoxicated.

PEER PRESSURE AND DRUG USE

The use of addictive substances by teenagers has been tracked for many years. This includes such items as tobacco products (cigarettes, cigars, and chew) and a variety of other illicit substances. In years past, advertising for tobacco was more directly aimed at teens and young adults. Certain regulations have limited this advertising, but teens are still exposed to the glamorization of cigarette use via many venues. This also holds true for "hardcore" drugs, which are often shown as glamorous on television and in movies. As a teenager, you are at increased risk for peer pressure to try drugs. Trying illicit substances can be especially harmful, as the addictive properties of drugs can begin after the first use. Details about some of the most common illicit items you may be pressured to try are listed below.

TOBACCO

Tobacco was first grown in the United States in the 1600s. It was associated with slavery and played a role in the start and financing of the Civil War. Initially, tobacco was used in pipes and for cigars, but in the mid-1800s it became popular in cigarette form. Although health risks were recognized as early as the 19th century from cigarettes, it was not until recent years that tobacco companies acknowledged the risks from smoking, and individual states began passing laws to restrict public smoking. In addition to cigarettes, both chewing tobacco (loose leaves of tobacco) and snuff (finely ground tobacco, often in small pouches that you place in your mouth) have been found to cause cancer.

Nicotine, the active ingredient in tobacco, is one of the most addictive substances known. People who try to quit smoking on their own have a 3% chance of success. Using items such as the nicotine patch or gum only increases the success rate by another 3%, to a total of 6%. Cigarettes have been associated with numerous health risks. These include high blood pressure, heart disease, and numerous cancers. These risks are the same for second-hand smokers—people who inhale cigarette smoke by virtue of being near those who are smoking. Most cigarette smokers begin their use of tobacco in their late teens and are often influenced by friends or family when they begin. Recent research shows that up to 90% or more of people who are smokers wish they could quit or that they had not started smoking in the first place. As a teenager facing the decision about whether to give in to peer pressure and try a cigarette, it will be important to

Not Everyone
Is Doing What You Think:
Data on Tobacco, Alcohol, and Drug Use Among Teens

The majority of teenagers disapprove of regular use of every type of tobacco, alcohol, or drug.

Item and Grade	Daily Use (%)	Used in Last 30 Days (%)
Cigarettes		
8th	3.1	6.8
10th	5.9	12.3
12th	11.4	20.4
Smokeless Tobacco		
8th	0.8	3.5
10th	1.4	5.0
12th	2.7	6.5
Marijuana		
8th	0.9	5.8
10th	2.7	13.8
12th	5.4	19.4
Hallucinogens		
8th	No Data	0.9
10th	No Data	1.3
12th	No Data	2.2
Ecstasy		
8th	No Data	0.8
10th	No Data	1.1
12th	No Data	1.8

Lifetime Use (used at least once in life) (%)	Change in Past 10 Years in Teen Lifetime Use (%)	Percentage of Teens Who Disapprove of Regular Use of Item
20.5	-25.2	86.7
31.7	-26.0	85.2
44.7	-20.6	80.5
9.8	-5.2	82.1
12.2	-10.5	81.8
15.6	-10.6	No Data
14.6	-7.6	86.8
29.9	-9.7	83.0
42.6	-6.5	79.6
3.3	-1.6	54.7
5.5	-4.3	69.8
8.7	-5.4	93.5
2.4	-0.3	66.5
4.3	-0.8	83.0
6.2	+0.4	88.2

(continues)

(continued)

Item and Grade	Daily Use (%)	Used in Last 30 Days (%)
Cocaine		
8th	No Data	0.8
10th	No Data	1.2
12th	No Data	1.9
Methamphetamine		
8th	No Data	0.7
10th	No Data	0.7
12th	No Data	0.6
Opioids other than Heroin		
8th	No Data	No Data
10th	No Data	No Data
12th	No Data	3.8
Alcohol		
8th	0.7	15.9
10th	1.0	28.8
12th	2.8	43.1

Source: National Institute on Drug Abuse, Monitoring the Future Survey, 2008

think carefully about the ramifications of what might seem to be a harmless act. Nicotine is a short-acting drug that creates withdrawal symptoms that may make it seem that you have the flu. Common withdrawal symptoms include cravings to smoke, headaches, stomachaches, shakiness, coughing, sore throat, problems sleeping, being irritable and cranky, and having a hard time concentrating. Some of these symptoms may be present even after the first time you have a cigarette or use chewing tobacco. With such a high number of people

Lifetime Use (used at least once in life) (%)	Change in Past 10 Years in Teen Lifetime Use (%)	Percentage of Teens Who Disapprove of Regular Use of Item
3.0	-1.6	90.1
4.5	-2.7	92.1
7.2	-2.1	94.8
2.3	-2.2	No Data
2.4	-4.9	No Data
2.8	-5.4	No Data
No Data	No Data	No Data
No Data	No Data	No Data
13.2	+3.4	No Data
38.9	-13.6	83.2
58.3	-11.5	77.2
71.9	-9.5	68.9

who wish they could quit versus how difficult it is to stop smoking, the best choice clearly is to never start.

MARIJUANA

Marijuana has been used for varied purposes for thousands of years. It is the most widely used illegal drug in the world today. In the United States, marijuana became illegal for use in the 1930s. Marijuana has been studied for many uses, and although it remains illegal on a national level, individual states have differing policies on its use.

The active ingredient in Marijuana is THC (delta-9-tetrahydrocannabinol). This substance produces mind-altering effects, and the content of THC in marijuana determines how strong the psychoactive effects of the plant are. Synthetic THC has been studied for medical use. There are many misconceptions regarding marijuana, and these misconceptions can lead to increased peer pressure to try it. You may hear comments such as "It can't hurt you; they give it to cancer and AIDS patients." It is important that you have accurate information about what exactly happens with marijuana use.

Marijuana poses a variety of health risks. When someone smokes marijuana, he or she experiences an increased heart rate, dry mouth and throat, and bloodshot eyes. Mentally, marijuana intoxication causes impaired concentration and memory, alterations in the sense of time, and a decrease in coordination. Marijuana use is also associated with "panic attacks," which are an extreme fear of "going crazy," with accelerated heart rate, confusion, sweating, and a feeling of impending death. These panic reactions usually necessitate a trip to the emergency room.

Although people argue that you cannot be addicted to marijuana, this is not true. Although there are no physical withdrawal symptoms (such as when you are addicted to alcohol, cocaine, or pain pills), you can become psychologically dependent on marijuana. People do develop tolerance to the effects of marijuana and begin to require more of the active ingredient (THC) to reach the same "high."

For teenagers, marijuana is especially dangerous. The impairment in focus, concentration, and motivation that comes from marijuana use can lead to devastating school problems, including dropping out. The younger you are when you start marijuana use, the more likely that you will experiment with other drugs as you get older. Marijuana causes a lack of interest not only in schoolwork but can affect your relationships with your family and friends and lead to isolation.

An extreme effect of marijuana is psychotic reactions (hearing voices, seeing things, or feeling that people are out to get you). Marijuana is often combined with other drugs and can be associated with life-altering events such as date rape and traffic accidents. Long-term use of marijuana is associated with many health risks, including cancer risks, heart and lung problems, and impaired fertility (making it harder to have children in the future).

ECSTASY

Ecstasy is a "designer-drug" made synthetically and rising in popularity, especially among teens. Ecstasy refers to 3, 4-methylenedioxymethamphetamine (MDMA) and was first popularized in use at all-night dance parties, or "raves," although in recent years it has been spreading to many more locations.

Ecstasy causes psychoactive effects when taken in pill form that last for several hours. It causes the immediate release of several neurotransmitters implicated in psychiatric disorders including serotonin, dopamine, and norepinephrine. The release of these neurotransmitters causes an increase in brain activity, which affects both physical and mental systems throughout the body.

When taking ecstasy, people experience confusion, anxiety, inability to sleep, and derealization or depersonalization (feelings that you are not part of your body). You may also feel depressed and paranoid. Physically, the rapid release of neurotransmitters causes muscle tension (including teeth clenching), nausea, vision problems, sweating or chills, and an increase in heart rate and blood pressure. Combining these symptoms with the popular use of MDMA at clubs and dances has led to fatalities throughout the United States. MDMA is often associated with the use of other drugs, and reports indicate that ecstasy, alcohol, and marijuana are often used together, increasing dangerous outcomes.

Ecstasy use is a major risk for teens, as youths may be given a pill for a different drug than what they think they are receiving. Two compounds that have been associated with fatal outcomes are sometimes sold as ecstasy. These are MDA (methylenedioxyamphetamine) and PMA (paramethocyamphetamine), both of which can produce feelings similar to ecstasy but are neurotoxic and can destroy brain cells. As with other drugs, teens are especially vulnerable to abuse situations, including date rape, when using ecstasy. The majority of people who present to an emergency room for MDMA complications are under the age of 25, indicating that use of the drug is mainly in teens and young adults. Although many teens believe that ecstasy is not addictive, there have been studies showing that users of ecstasy did meet criteria for addictive behaviors. These behaviors included using the drug despite knowing it was harmful, having withdrawal effects from not taking the drug, and developing tolerance—needing to use higher quantities to get the same high.

METHAMPHETAMINE

Methamphetamine, also known as speed, crystal, and glass, is a very addictive stimulant drug that affects the central nervous system. It is a white, odorless powder that is usually snorted, smoked, or injected into the body. Methamphetamine was first synthesized at the beginning of the 20th century. Although methamphetamine is available as a prescription drug, it has limited uses, and methamphetamine bought from the street has much higher levels of active drug than via prescription.

Methamphetamine increases the release of the neurotransmitter dopamine, which is a common mechanism of action for drugs of abuse. Taking even small amounts of methamphetamine causes problems sleeping, decreased appetite, increased respiration, rapid heart rate, a rise in blood pressure, and even stroke. The effects of methamphetamine last for six to eight hours and are followed by a period of withdrawal that includes intense cravings for more of the drug and that may lead to more extreme health effects, including confusion, anxiety, violent behavior, and psychosis (including feeling paranoid and having hallucinations). As with other drugs, methamphetamine causes impaired judgment and can lead to unsafe behavior with lifelong consequences.

Methamphetamine, along with cocaine, is a main cause of trips to the emergency room for both psychiatric and medical issues. Chronic use of methamphetamine can result in permanent psychosis, similar to having the illness schizophrenia, which has devastating consequences.

COCAINE

Cocaine is a highly addictive drug first synthesized in the 1860's. Originally, it was experimented with as a treatment for many medical conditions. The addictive qualities of cocaine were discovered soon after its use as a medicine began. It was available for sale over the counter in the United States until 1916, when it was banned. It is used rarely today as an anesthetic and is recognized as a major cause of pain and suffering throughout the world.

Cocaine is usually snorted or dissolved in water and injected directly into your veins. Crack is a form of cocaine that comes in a rock crystal that is heated to produce vapors that are inhaled. The intensity and duration of the effects of cocaine depend on how the drug is administered. The faster cocaine is absorbed into the bloodstream leads to a more intense high. More intense highs last for a very short time, such as five to 10 minutes from smoking, to 15 to 30 minutes from snorting. In order to maintain the high, you must administer the drug again at a higher dose. This feature of cocaine makes it extremely addictive and difficult to treat once you are addicted.

As with methamphetamine, cocaine increases brain levels of dopamine, a brain chemical associated with pleasure and movement. Normally, dopamine is released by a neuron (a certain type of brain cell) and then gets recycled back into the cell that released it. Cocaine prevents the dopamine from being recycled, causing excessive amounts of dopamine to build up and cause a high. This pattern leads to addiction.

Cocaine has many negative effects on your body. Cocaine causes constriction of blood vessels and an increase in temperature, heart rate, and blood pressure. It also causes stomach pain and nausea. Binge cocaine use leads to restlessness, anxiety, irritability, and violence. As with methamphetamine, cocaine can cause psychosis, in which you lose touch with reality. Cocaine has been documented to cause acute cardiovascular and cerebrovascular emergencies, such as heart attacks and stroke. These findings have been found in young people with no history of any heart problems.

Cocaine addiction is difficult to treat. Teens who become addicted to cocaine often resort to stealing from family, friends, and anyone else to get money for their habit. Cocaine addiction does not have as many good treatment options as alcohol, pain pills, or even tobacco, and people addicted to cocaine universally regret the decision they made to try it in the first place.

PRESCRIPTION DRUGS

Prescription drug use is a growing area of concern for teens. After marijuana, prescription pills are the most commonly abused illicit drug of teens. Although many medications can be abused, there are three types of medicines that are most often abused. These are opioids (usually prescribed to treat pain), central nervous system depressants (used to treat anxiety and sleep disorders), and stimulant medications (prescribed to treat attention-deficit hyperactivity disorder and narcolepsy).

Opioids. Opioids are prescribed primarily for treatment of pain, both acute (short-term) and chronic (long-term). The names of some common opioid medicines include Vicodin, OxyContin, Percocet, morphine, codeine, and fentanyl. When prescribed and used according to direction, the medications relieve suffering for many individuals and do not pose a large risk of addiction. However, when the medicines are taken in either greater quantities than intended or ingested through other means than intended (for example, by crushing and snorting or injecting the medicine), then you are more likely to become addicted and have many adverse reactions.

Opioids produce drowsiness, constipation, and, of most concern, can cause respiratory depression. This means that if you take a large single dose of one of the medicines, you can stop your breathing and thereby kill yourself. Combining opioid medicines with other drugs, especially alcohol, can magnify these effects and increase your risk of death. With regular use of opioids, your body will become addicted. Withdrawal symptoms from the medications include feeling restless, muscle and bone pain, diarrhea and vomiting, and involuntary movements. These uncomfortable withdrawal symptoms lead opioid users to frantically search for more of the drug, sacrificing money, friendships, schoolwork, and everything else to obtain the next high.

Central nervous system depressants. Known as barbiturates and benzodiazepines, these medicines work by slowing normal brain function. They are often used to treat sleep disorders, anxiety disorders, and some neurological disorders, including epilepsy. Some of the more common of these medicines include Valium, Xanax, Mebaral, and Nembutal. Many people abuse these medicines to counteract the effects of other illicit drugs, including cocaine and amphetamine.

Similar to opioid pain medicines, central nervous system depressants can be highly addictive and produce severe withdrawal symptoms. With acute use, the medicines cause drowsiness, and if combined with alcohol, opioid medicines, or even some over-the-counter cold pills, they can slow your heart rate and breathing and cause death. People who have been using these medicines chronically are at high risk for developing seizures and dying if they are discontinued abruptly. Stopping these medicines always require the supervision of a physician and often time in the hospital.

Stimulants. *Stimulants* refers to amphetamines (Adderall and Dexedrine) and methylphenidates (Ritalin). These drugs work by increasing levels of the neurotransmitters dopamine and norepinephrine. Because they affect dopamine, which mediates the pleasure response in your body, they can produce a sense of euphoria and are subject to abuse. In addition to euphoria, stimulants cause an increase in blood pressure, heart rate, and blood sugar. They can help with alertness, attention, and energy if used properly and are used to treat diseases such as attention-deficit hyperactivity disorder and narcolepsy.

Stimulants can be abused by taking the medicines orally, but many times people crush or dissolve the tablets and snort the contents or inject them into their blood vessels. Injecting stimulants is especially dangerous, as they do not dissolve well when heated in water, and small particles can clog blood vessels if injected. When prescribed by a physician, stimulants are started in low doses and gradually increased if needed. When abused, stimulants are taken in large doses, causing rapid release of neurotransmitters (similar to methamphetamines), which disrupts the normal communication between brain cells and can lead to addiction. As with methamphetamine use, taking stimulants can cause a rapid and irregular heartbeat, high body temperature, seizures, irritability, and psychosis.

HALLUCINOGENS

Hallucinogens are a class of drugs that interfere with the action or binding of different neurotransmitters (including serotonin, catecholamines, and acetylcholine) and cause alterations in the perception of reality. The exact mechanism of how hallucinogens work remains unclear. The most common hallucinogens are LSD (lysergic acid diethylamide), PCP (phencyclidine), and psilocybin, which is obtained from certain types of mushrooms. Unlike most other drugs, the effects of hallucinogens are extremely variable and unreliable and produce drastically different effects in different people. This is due to the variability in the amount of active compound that is present in each type of drug. These features make the use of hallucinogens particularly dangerous.

Hallucinogens cause a variety of physical effects, in addition to the psychological effects described below. You may experience increased body temperature, heart rate, blood pressure, and sweating when using hallucinogens. You may also have tremors, muscle relaxation or weakness, nausea, vomiting, and shallow breathing with the use of any hallucinogen.

LSD. LSD comes in several forms, including tablets, capsules, and liquid. Sometimes it is added to paper, decorated, and divided into pieces. LSD "trips" often last a long time, and it can take you more than 12 hours to stop hallucinating. LSD disrupts the neurotransmitter serotonin and other interactions between nerve cells. When using LSD, your mood state may swing rapidly from one emotion to another, such as feeling extremely happy one minute and then feeling extremely depressed the next. LSD can make you feel delusional (that people are trying to hurt you or that you have superhuman powers) and cause visual hallucinations (seeing things that are not real). Your sense of time is altered. You will experience depersonalization (a sense that you are not in your body) and derealization (a sense that the world is not real), which can both be terrifying experiences and lead to dangerous outcomes. You may experience these terrifying thoughts and feel that you are losing control, going insane, or dying. People who have used LSD are also subjected to "flashbacks." There have been flashbacks documented both a few days after use and sometimes as late as one year after using LSD. At times, the flashbacks persist and may lead to a psychiatric diagnosis known as hallucinogen-induced persisting perceptual disorder. This may require you to take medicines to control your lingering symptoms from LSD use.

Mushrooms. Psilocybin mushrooms are either consumed when fresh or dried and usually by mouth. They are often brewed in tea or cooked with other foods to hide their flavor, leading to many teens consuming them without knowing. The effects of mushrooms usually last six hours and are similar to LSD. There are many species of mushrooms, some of which can be lethal (usually by causing severe liver damage) in a very short time period. There have been cases of people not identifying mushrooms correctly and instead of getting high causing profound liver damage and death. The usual health effects of mushrooms include changes in motor reflexes, sweating and heart rate, behavior, and perception of the world. You can experience hallucinations and an inability to discern fantasy from reality. As with LSD, you may experience panic reactions and psychosis. Mushrooms also put you at risk for flashbacks, psychiatric illness, and impaired memory.

PCP. PCP is a white powder that dissolves in water or alcohol. It is easily mixed with coloring agents and is usually consumed as tablets, capsules, or colored powder. Unlike LSD or mushrooms, PCP is commonly snorted or smoked, in addition to being ingested orally. PCP can be applied to marijuana, often without teenagers' knowledge. Although it is not completely known how PCP affects the brain, we do know that it causes changes different from mushrooms or LSD. PCP works mainly through a glutamate receptor in the brain. This receptor is important for your perception of pain, your memory, and how you respond to your environment. PCP was used as an anesthetic until 1965, when the side effects from its controlled use were felt to outweigh its benefits. Patients often became agitated, delusional, and irrational. As with LSD, PCP can cause dissociation, making you feel that you are detached from either your body or your environment. Teens who abuse PCP are often attracted to the feelings of strength, invulnerability, and "numbing" sensation to the mind. PCP has been associated with disastrous outcomes. PCP can make you appear schizophrenic, causing hallucinations, delusions, paranoia, and an inability to discern what is real in your environment. PCP also gives you mood disturbances and increases your risk for being arrested or brought into a medical or psychiatric emergency room and with long-term use causes memory loss, depression, and cognitive problems. Unlike mushrooms and LSD, PCP is physiologically addictive and can cause you to spend all of your time, money, and resources to satisfy your craving for the drug.

WHAT'S THE BIG DEAL WITH DRUG USE?

Most teenagers are not aware of the societal costs of drug use. Although you may hear comments such as "You are not hurting anyone by using a little dope," the drug trade is arguably responsible for more suffering throughout the United States and the world than anything else. Untreated substance abuse and addiction add significant costs to families and communities, including those related to violence and property crimes, prison expenses, court and criminal costs, emergency room visits, health care use, child abuse and neglect, lost child support, foster care and welfare costs, reduced productivity, and unemployment. The National Institute of Drug Abuse reports that the cost to society of illicit drug abuse alone is $181 billion annually. When combined with alcohol and tobacco use, the costs exceed $500 billion, including health care, criminal justice, and lost productivity. The majority of drug, alcohol, and tobacco abuses begin during teenage years. Learning to say "no" to drug use in peer pressure situations does more than help you as an individual, it helps our society as well.

PEER PRESSURE AND SEXUAL ACTIVITY

All teens are in an intense phase of growth, mediated by changes in hormones throughout the body. A normal part of these changes includes an increase in thoughts and curiosity regarding sexual activity. With the growth of the Internet, for better or for worse, teens now have easy access to materials of a sexual nature, including extreme examples of sexual behavior. Although most teens are able to filter this material properly, the intense exposure via advertising, movies, television, and the Internet to sexual activity may complicate the peer pressure situation for teens. As a teenager, the biggest concern is that poorly planned sexual behavior can lead to an outcome that can drastically alter your life. Peer pressure comments about sex often include false information regarding pregnancy and sexually transmitted disease issues. Examples of erroneous comments may include "You can't get pregnant during your period" or "You can't get a sexually transmitted disease through oral sex."

TEEN PREGNANCY

Nothing is more disruptive to the life of a teenager than becoming pregnant. Teen pregnancy is associated with failure to complete school, domestic violence, and psychiatric illness, including depression and anxiety. Although the teen pregnancy rate had been declining throughout the 1990s up to 2004, there was an increase in teen pregnancy rates in 2005 and 2006, raising concerns among many health agencies. Teens who become pregnant experience a range of emotional responses that are difficult to handle. You may feel embarrassed, scared, helpless, hopeless, depressed, and anxious. These emotions may make it difficult for you to speak with your parents or other adults who may be able to provide assistance. Teens with unwanted pregnancies may have poor outcomes when they try to handle everything on their own.

SEXUALLY TRANSMITTED DISEASES

Teens are at higher risk for contracting sexually transmitted diseases (STDs) than other age groups. You can acquire an STD through any intimate contact, not just through sexual intercourse. You may feel protected from contracting an STD because you think that your partner has never had any intimate contact with another person, only to find out that they have not been honest with you. You may feel that as long as there are no obvious sores, lesions, or bumps on your partner that you are safe, but STDs can be transmitted when there are no physical signs. In fact, many teens who transmit STDs are not even aware that they are infected. You may think that if you get an STD it is no big deal and you can just take a few antibiotic pills to get rid of it, but this is also not true. Some STDs have lifelong consequences that include damaging your ability to have a baby in the future, causing recurrent symptoms throughout your life (Herpes) or even death (from HIV/AIDS).

Herpes. Herpes refers to two different viruses, herpes simplex virus 1 (HSV-1) and herpes simplex virus 2 (IISV-2). HSV-1 is the virus that causes cold sores around your mouth but can also infect your genital region. HSV-2 is the virus most commonly associated with genital herpes. Herpes is a sexually transmitted disease that can cause sores in the oral, anal, or genital region. Some people who are exposed to the virus may never have an outbreak yet still be able to spread the disease to their partners. It is suspected that as many as one in four or five people in the United States are infected with herpes.

Herpes causes sores that are often painful and irritating. You may experience flulike symptoms, including swelling of your lymph nodes and general body aches during an outbreak. These symptoms are usually worst during your first outbreak. The symptoms go away after one to two weeks, but the virus remains in your body. At this time, there is no cure for genital herpes, although there is medication that can help decrease the recurrence of the sores and provide some relief from the physical symptoms. Herpes can cause severe illness, including death, to newborns, and thus it is important for women to be aware of whether they have this illness and to discuss it with their doctor. The only 100% sure way to avoid herpes is abstinence, which is avoiding any sexual contact. Proper use of latex condoms during intercourse or dental dams during oral sex can greatly reduce your risk for contracting any STD.

Syphilis. Syphilis is a sexually transmitted disease caused by bacteria rather than a virus. Before antibiotic medicines were invented, syphilis was responsible for an enormous amount of suffering throughout the world. Since antibiotics have been in existence, syphilis has been in steady decline. However, in the last few years there has been an increase in the number of syphilis cases. The first sign that you have syphilis is the appearance of red, firm sores in the genital, oral, or anal region. These sores are painless, and because of this people often do not realize they are infected. The sores go away after a few weeks, but if the disease has not been treated, it will continue to get worse. The next stage of syphilis involves flu-like symptoms and a rash that can appear on the soles of your feet and palms of your hands. Sometimes these symptoms are mild, and people are not aware that they have any type of infection. After these symptoms resolve in one to two weeks, syphilis enters a latent phase. In this phase, the infection is hidden, even though it is still present. The disease can remain hidden like this for many years. The final stage of syphilis includes tertiary syphilis, in which the bacterial infection spreads throughout the body. You can be infected in your heart, brain, spinal cord, and bones. Symptoms from these infections include problems walking, feeling numb, blindness, and even death. No matter what, if you have any concerns that you may be infected with syphilis, you should see a doctor as soon as possible for treatment. Women who have unknown syphilis can cause severe birth defects in their children.

Genital warts (HPV). Genital warts are warts that appear in the genital area for both males and females. Warts can appear in many shapes but are usually flesh-colored, raised bumps. Sometimes they are hard to see, and many times people don't know they are infected. Genital warts are caused by a virus known as human papilloma virus (HPV). There are more than 30 different types of HPV. Genital warts are transmitted through intimate contact. They are very common in young adults and teens, with some estimates as high as 50% of people being infected.

Genital warts may get bigger or increase in numbers if untreated. Genital warts are most problematic for females, as they can increase your risk for cancer. The most common concern is regarding cervical cancer. HPV can cause problems with the cervix (the opening to the uterus located at the top of the vagina) that may lead to cervical cancer.

Chlamydia. Chlamydia is a sexually transmitted disease caused by a bacterium, *Chlamydia trachomatis.* Chlamydia is a very common sexually transmitted disease and can lead to pelvic inflammatory disease in girls, which can cause fertility problems later in life. Chlamydia infections occur through sexual contact, and chlamydia infections can also occur in your eyes if you touch bodily fluids with the bacteria and then touch your eye. As with other sexually transmitted diseases, it can be difficult to know if you have an infection. Symptoms may include a discharge from the vagina in females or from the urethra (the tip of the penis where urine comes out) in males. In females there may be bleeding in between menstrual cycles, pain in the lower abdomen, or pain during urination. Males may have pain during urination and may get swollen testicles.

Treatment for chlamydia involves taking antibiotic medicine. The danger with a chlamydia infection, as with other STDs, is that if it goes untreated for a long period of time you can have serious health problems.

Gonorrhea. Gonorrhea is another bacterial STD caused by *Neisseria gonorrhoeae.* Many of its symptoms are very similar to chlamydia. In girls gonorrhea may cause a yellow-green vaginal discharge or pain with urination. As with chlamydia, there may also be bleeding in between menstrual cycles. Gonorrhea, if left untreated, can also cause pelvic inflammatory disease. Gonorrhea in boys is usually more noticeable, with pain on urination and a yellow-white discharge from the urethra. If left untreated, gonorrhea can cause serious problems for males and females, including fertility issues with men as well as women. Gonorrhea is treated by taking a course of antibiotic medication.

Human immunodeficiency virus (HIV). There are currently 42 million people in the world living with HIV or the disease it causes, acquired immunodeficiency syndrome (AIDS). HIV is a virus that attacks a type of cell in the body (CD4 helper cell) that plays an important role in protecting us from disease. As HIV destroys these cells, our bodies can no longer fight off disease, and this leads to the diagnosis of AIDS. Compared to other diseases, HIV is very recent, being first discovered in the 1980s. Because of the tremendous amount of suffering associated with HIV and AIDS, there is a lot of research in progress to find new treatments for the disease, although at this time there is still no cure.

HIV is transmitted in several ways. In addition to sexual contact (via oral, vaginal, or anal sex), the disease can be transmitted through needles (used to inject drugs or for tattooing). People with other sexually transmitted diseases are at higher risk for contracting HIV.

When your immune system is weakened from HIV, you lose the ability to fight off infections and begin to contract multiple illnesses. As each illness wears down your body further, you tend to get more unable to fight off future infections, leading to a rapid decline in function and death.

As with other sexually transmitted diseases, you may not know that you have contracted HIV for many years. Some people may go for up to 10 years without having any symptoms. During this time, you may be spreading HIV to other people unknowingly. In addition, there is no way to tell that someone else has HIV without getting a blood test. (In other words, people may look completely normal and healthy yet still be infected.)

Since HIV is incurable and can lead to death, it is important for teens to be prepared to resist peer pressure to engage in sexual activities that you may not be prepared for. It is also important to know current information on all STDs and how to protect yourself from acquiring them.

RAPE

Rape is forced, unwanted sexual intercourse and happens to both males and females. Teens are more vulnerable to rape when they have been using drugs or alcohol or find themselves without friends in dangerous or unknown environments. Rapists use real or threatened violence to force sexual behavior on the victim. Rape can happen by strangers, acquaintances, friends, or even family members. Date rape is, unfortunately, a common occurrence among teens and indicates that you know who your attacker is. Peer pressure may lead you to put yourself in a dangerous situation in which you are more likely to be attacked.

The consequences of rape can be severe and lifelong. In addition to leading to possible unwanted pregnancies or sexually transmitted diseases, rapes can lead to years of depression and anxiety and post-traumatic stress disorder (PTSD). Many teens who have been raped never tell anyone, leading to increased emotional distress for many years after the trauma.

PEER PRESSURE AND FIGHTING

Nelson was one of the strongest kids at his high school. He had been on the wrestling team since his freshman year and performed well at his team meets. Now in his junior year, Nelson was an avid supporter of all his high school's teams, and often he and his friends would travel to away games to support the school's basketball team. After one particularly intense game in which his school lost by two points, Nelson and his friends encountered a group of students from the opposing school while walking to their cars in the parking lot. The other students made a few snide comments about how their school "sucked" and that they probably wouldn't win any more games this year. Nelson was usually able to ignore similar comments, and although he felt bitter over his team's loss, he continued on to his car. Regrettably, the taunting continued. The ringleader from the opposing school's group of teens started heading over to Nelson and his friends. As his comments continued, Nelson's friends began to pressure Nelson to react. Nelson was clearly taller and stronger than this other kid, and his friends wanted Nelson to "teach him a lesson." Ultimately, when the other teen made a rude gesture to Nelson, he lost control. Nelson quickly tackled the other student to the ground and began to pummel him. The other student was not able to defend himself and was quickly knocked unconscious. Because the basketball game had just let out, there were many people around, and adults quickly intervened. Nelson had injured the other student so severely that he needed to go to the hospital. In addition, the police came and arrested Nelson on assault and battery charges. As he was being handcuffed and placed into the police car, Nelson began to realize how serious a mistake he had made.

Peer pressure is a leading contributor to violent behavior in teens. Being together with a group of friends can lead to a loss of good judgment when handling situations that may lead to physical altercations. Adding in any use of alcohol or drugs can magnify this problem. For Nelson, peer pressure caused a loss of judgment and had devastating consequences for him. He not only had to spend time in juvenile hall for his assault but also received a school suspension, and this resulted in a loss of his spot on the wrestling team, jeopardizing his plans for a college scholarship. The parents of the teenager who was hospitalized filed a civil lawsuit that threatened to exhaust the life savings of Nelson's parents. None of Nelson's friends faced similar consequences for encouraging him to fight.

Using the strategies from chapter 2, you should practice thinking about situations you may find yourself in and explore which options exist to handle the peer pressure without coming to harm. Be wary of engaging in violent behavior—the court system does not consider "But my friends told me to" a valid excuse for any illegal behavior.

STRATEGIES FOR HANDLING DANGEROUS SITUATIONS

This chapter has discussed many of the serious consequences of peer pressure. By reading this book, you are increasing your awareness of peer pressure situations. This increased awareness can help you avoid many of the above negative outcomes. In every situation in which you begin to feel scared, it is helpful to have resources you can use to protect yourself. Depending on his or her friends, family, neighborhood, etc., each teen will have his or her own algorithm, or step-by-step plan, to help when peer pressure situations escalate beyond what he or she can handle alone. There are three main groups of people to think about when you are in need of aid.

PARENTS

Regardless of your relationship with your parents, it is an almost universal truth that no parent wants his or her child to suffer. As children become teens, it is recommended that parents establish policies of open, honest communication without fear of being judged on the part of the teenager. Many parents are scared to engage in these discussions with their kids, and if this is the case in your family, you should feel free to initiate the conversation with your parents. One advantage of recent times is that almost all teens have quick access to their parents through cell phones or text messaging. Depending on the situation you are in, notifying your parents that you need help can save you from harm. Many teen deaths could be avoided each year if teens would give their parents a call when they are in tough situations. Unfortunately, many teens tend to risk their lives just to avoid being embarrassed, getting in trouble, or disappointing their parents. A common example of this situation presents itself at many parties. You may have a curfew that you need to honor or face consequences, such as losing your cell phone or car privileges or being grounded. If you are not safe to drive or if the people you went to the party with are no longer safe to drive, many teens do not think about the much more tragic consequences that may occur by getting in a car with someone who is intoxicated from drugs or alcohol. Rather than worrying about death, you may want to risk getting home in an unsafe manner to avoid much more minor consequences. Most parents are happy to come get their child, and the maturity that you show by being able to call your parents usually leads to positive rather than negative outcomes.

To decrease the chances that you will make an unsafe decision, speak to your parents ahead of time, and get an emergency safety plan in place. If you are in a situation where your parents are unable to be supportive, there is usually another caregiver (such as another family member, older brother or sister, or adult friend) who can be contacted for help in dangerous situations. If this is the case for you, think about the caregivers in your life, identify one or more of them ahead of time, and talk with them about being able to help you in emergency situations.

FRIENDS

Although parents or caregivers are usually the best option for providing assistance when in danger, you may be able to look to your friends as another support system. When in dangerous peer pressure situations, such as when drugs, unwanted sexual activity, or alcohol are involved, you may be able to reach one or more of your friends for assistance. As with your parents, identifying which of your friends are best suited to help you in times of crisis and then speaking with them about "backing each other up" can prepare you for emergencies.

POLICE

In the United States, we are fortunate to have quick access to the police and other emergency services with a simple phone call. Although it may not seem like an emergency if you are stranded at a party without a safe ride home, the police or other emergency service teams can often provide other avenues for support. Many communities have a safe-ride program whereby teens can get rides home when needed, and the police usually have the contact information for these agencies. Whenever there is a threat of violence, unwanted sexual activity, or substance abuse, having the ability to call the police can often immediately end the danger.

WHAT YOU NEED TO KNOW

- ▶ Peer pressure can lead teens to participate in many dangerous activities.
- ▶ Alcohol use causes health problems and is responsible for the deaths of many teens through drunk driving accidents.

- Tobacco use usually starts when people are teenagers and is highly addictive, and almost all who are current smokers wish they had never started smoking in the first place.
- Marijuana is a common drug of abuse among teens, causing problems with focus, concentration, and motivation as well as many harmful effects to your health.
- Ecstasy is a synthetic drug that can be addictive and has led to fatalities.
- Methamphetamines and cocaine are highly addictive drugs that cause dangerous cardiovascular side effects.
- Prescription drugs are rising in use among teens. The improper use of prescription drugs leads to addiction and negative health effects, including death.
- Hallucinogens cause a loss of a sense of reality, and teens are often not aware of how much of the drug they are taking when using them.
- Teens are more likely to experience bad outcomes from sexual activity due to peer pressure. These include pregnancy, sexually transmitted diseases, and rape.
- Physical fights and violence are often precipitated by peer pressure, sometimes with devastating consequences.
- Teens who develop strategies ahead of time for handling dangerous situations are more likely to emerge without serious harm from these peer pressure situations.
- It is important to know who to contact in cases of emergencies, including parents, caregivers, friends, or police.

4 ▐▌▌

Who Are Your Friends, Really?

Cole was new to Vista Mountain High School. He started off with a group of friends who hung out in the academic quad. They were pretty nice kids, but Cole decided that he wanted to join a different group. This group hung out in the rally court on campus and was viewed by everyone as the "top of the food chain." The group consisted of the coolest kids: the jocks, the cheerleaders, and the most popular party-goers. Cole felt that he could "make it" into that group, so one day he braved it and walked up to the group in the rally court. The group seemed to react well to Cole's arrival; there were no explicit rejections or cold shoulders of any kind.

Within two days of joining the group, just as Cole was getting comfortable, some guy in the group threw a trash can over Cole. The kids laughed at the pitiful scene of the new boy being stuck under an overturned trash can. Piles of food wrappers, ketchup-laden paper plates, and miscellaneous debris from countless rally lunches landed on his head and fell down his torso. In addition, the weight of the trash can left his head aching. Just as he was making sense of what had happened—just as he was beginning to push the trash can with all its stench off of him—the bell rang, and lunch was over. The snickering boys went off to their fifth period before Cole had a chance to protest.

Despite this humiliating incident, Cole returned to the rally court group the next day. He figured that this was just a test to see how "tough" he was. Although he was really angry at the injustice and embarrassment of the trash can incident, Cole was determined to show this group that he had the brazen confidence to not let the incident scare him away. That day, another trash can was thrown onto Cole. This time he quickly regrouped and flung the trash can off his body. With rage in his eyes, he confronted the guy who threw it on him and screamed out protests about how bad a thing he was doing. In fact, Cole drew up the nerve to start a fight with him and condemn him openly for the act. The girls in the group showed support for Cole, agreeing with him that the boys were being ridiculously cruel. Nevertheless, a week later Cole was hit with a baseball bat. Cole then took the bat and chased the boy around with it.

After a few weeks had passed, it was apparent that the horrid abuse toward Cole had stopped. Within a few months, Cole knew that he had officially "made it" into the group. They started regularly inviting him to parties and saved places for him in the school assemblies, rallies, and football games. Just as Cole began to feel comfortable with the group, he was asked to throw a pizza into a new guy's face. Cole felt very uncomfortable with this and tried to coolly protest. However, he felt pressure to do it in order to remain in the group. Although he felt ashamed of himself, Cole was rounded up by the group ringleaders to perform an act of violence. He was now the perpetrator, after having finished in the role of victim. Once this new guy was accepted into the group, Cole was violence-free for a while, but he always wondered if these so-called friends really were interested in being a friend or just a social group that demanded its new members undergo pain in order to "make it." Would friends really want to put other friends through that? He would always wonder.

THE IMPORTANCE OF FRIENDS

One of the most protective factors while growing up is having several healthy friendships from elementary school throughout high school and adulthood. Having friendships helps you avoid problems with many tough issues that teenagers face. Some of the most important areas include:

- ► Mental health: Teens who do not have at least one friendship are more likely to suffer mental health symptoms. You are more likely to experience symptoms of depression and anxiety.
- ► Substance abuse: Teens without friendships are at higher risk for engaging in substance abuse for two reasons. First, you are more likely to give in to peer pressure in an effort to make new

Core Value Checklist

Below is a list of commonly held core values. At the bottom are some spaces to write in values that may not be listed but are important to you. Spend some time ranking the values, from highest to lowest, to help get a sense of what is important to you. Knowing your core values will help match you to friends with similar beliefs.

Value	Ranking
Respect	
Honesty	
Education	
Avoiding drug use	
Avoiding alcohol use	
Intelligence	
Drive to succeed	
Family	
Kindness	
Ability to be flexible	
Humor	
Staying calm	
Staying healthy	
Responsibility	
Integrity	
Compassion	

friends. Second, you are unlikely to have friends who can back you up when you are under pressure.

> Academics: Teens without friends tend to have worse school performances than their classmates.

In addition to the more serious issues listed above, friendships contribute to essential parts of maturing. For teenagers, your peer group is the number one influence on your behavior. Friendships allow the practicing of conflict resolution skills, including learning how to end an argument yet still remain friends. Friendships give you extra people to seek advice from, help you develop loyalty, and help you to practice giving and receiving support in times of need. As you get older, it is through your friendships that you identify what type of person you are, what your goals are for the future, and who you want to spend your time with. Friendships are also closely linked to self-esteem and confidence, which are perhaps the most important traits for predicting success in life as an adult.

CHOOSING FRIENDS WISELY

Despite the benefits of having multiple friendships, it doesn't mean that you should indiscriminately try to become friends with everyone you meet. There is a balance you must strike between being respectful to a person yet not feeling that you *need* to be that person's friend. Almost all teens have heard of the golden rule, which basically says to treat others as you would expect to be treated yourself. This is an appropriate guideline to follow in how you treat others, regardless of whether you desire to be their friend.

How can you know which friendships will be beneficial and not cause you harm? As mentioned earlier, once you are a teenager, you will have a core set of values that are being shaped from multiple sources. It is a good idea to think about the core values you hold highest and those that are less important to you. Keeping your core values in mind will allow you to "match" yourself with peers who are likely to be good fits as friends. It is important to remember that core values are different from interests or activities. There are many teens who have friends with very few common interests but the same set of core values. These friendships can be especially rewarding, as you gain exposure to new activities that may turn out to have positive benefits.

When you are in elementary school, your parents have a high level of control over your friendships. Although there are usually no limits on who you hang out with at school, when you are younger you tend to rely on your parents for transportation and interactions with peers outside of school. This changes as you become a teenager for several reasons. First, you are no longer reliant on your parents for transportation to meet your friends. Even if you are not driving, most teens are allowed to go places without being supervised. Riding your bike, skateboard, or scooter; taking the bus; or even walking places gives you increased freedom to choose who you want to spend your time with. Second, most parents no longer expect to meet the parents of your friends before you are allowed to get together with them. Although ultimately your parents may intervene in a friendship if there are clear, dangerous behaviors resulting from your spending time with a certain individual, by the time you become a teenager, it is your decision about who you are going to choose as your friends.

Given this responsibility, it is essential for you to know that your behavior will be influenced by your friends more than by any other source. After thinking about your core values and what you would like to accomplish in the future, work to find friends who match these goals. There are few teens who would state that they want to spend their lives using drugs or alcohol or wind up in jail or unemployed. Almost universally, teens would like to finish high school, go to college, and find a career that is rewarding. Sometimes teens feel that these goals are impossible (which is never the case) and spend more and more time engaged in behaviors that sabotage their future plans. When you lose focus on your life goals, you become susceptible to alcohol and drug abuse as ways to provide brief "escapes" from your current situation. Students in these situations try to find others to join them in their activities to make them feel better about giving up on their future. This is one group of people to avoid in choosing friendships.

In thinking about choosing your friendships, you may want to consider the following groups of teens, who participate in activities that predict success in the future.

ACADEMICS
Teens who take pride in their schoolwork and performance in class and have aspirations to attain further education after high school usually are on a trajectory that will lead to the fulfillment of positive life goals. By the time you are a freshman, most of your peers will have figured out their goals regarding education, so it is usually easy to determine whose educational plans match with yours.

EXTRACURRICULAR ACTIVITIES
Students who engage in extracurricular activities are more likely to be successful both academically and personally. These activities can be school based or community based.

ATHLETICS

Teens who participate in sports, either through their schools or through clubs outside their schools, are less likely to use drugs or alcohol and have an increased likelihood to complete high school and attend college. Participating in athletic activities does not always necessarily mean that you have to belong to a team. Teens who exercise regularly on their own, whether it be at health clubs or through activities such as running, biking, skateboarding, or skiing, also are more successful in school and at avoiding drug and alcohol use.

DRUG AND ALCOHOL USE

One of the best predictors for success in later life is whether teens engage in regular use of drugs or alcohol. Students who seem preoccupied with conversations about drugs or with obtaining and using drugs or alcohol have the highest rate of school failure and highest likelihood of ending up unemployed or in jail. Making a decision to avoid associating with your peers who appear headed down this path is probably the most important decision you can make when choosing friends.

WHEN TO END A FRIENDSHIP

T. J. was a tall, athletic, confident 10th grader who prided himself on being friends with everyone at school. He was fortunate to have spent his elementary school, middle school, and first two years of high school in the same house. He had a large group of friends when he moved to his middle school, and they had remained a cohesive group. Two members of the group, Victor and Jason, had begun experimenting with alcohol and marijuana in ninth grade. T. J. noticed that they no longer put the same effort into their schoolwork and was worried about their future. Jason, who formerly was an outstanding cross-country runner, was no longer interested in staying in shape or joining the track team. Victor, already somewhat shy, became more withdrawn and always seemed focused on getting his next high.

To their credit, Victor and Jason did not put pressure on T. J. or anyone else to try smoking marijuana or drinking alcohol. T. J.'s house was a popular destination for his friends because his parents kept the refrigerator and pantry stocked with food, and T. J.'s father was a "computer nerd" who converted one of the basement rooms of the house into a 12-computer linked network for gaming. T. J., who felt it important to maintain all of his friendships, often invited his friends, including Victor and Jason, over to his house to play on his dad's computer network. Because T. J. had never violated the rules regarding computer use (keeping the area clean, no drugs or alcohol allowed, and no downloading material from the Internet), he was given free access to the area by his father. T. J. made sure that everyone who ever came over was aware of these rules and the consequences he would face if they were violated.

One Saturday, T. J. arranged a gaming session at his house. Victor, Jason, and five other classmates descended on the computer room for an evening of snacks and team first-person shooter gaming. Although T. J. noticed that Victor and Jason had brought in sports drinks, he was not aware that half of the liquid in the drinks was vodka. As the night went on, Victor and Jason began acting more and more out of control. At one point, when Jason's character was shot down by the opposing team, he threw a can of soda at the player, which missed him and instead smashed into one of the expensive flat-screen monitors in the room, igniting sparks that sent a power surge through the network. At this point, it became clear to T. J. that Jason and Victor had been drinking alcohol, and as T. J. heard his father descending into the basement, he knew that their actions had just eliminated the possibility of future gaming sessions for T. J. and his friends.

No one likes to end friendships. As a teenager this is especially true, as there are extra fears that come with telling someone you no longer can hang out with them. You may have concerns that they will begin spreading rumors about you or try to get common friends to "choose sides." Ultimately, you need to balance the pros and cons of your friendships and decide when the negatives of hanging out with someone begin to outweigh the positive benefits of a friendship.

There are many reasons that can lead one to question the benefit of a friendship. Sometimes, as we will discuss in the next chapter, when you become aware that you are being bullied or victimized by one of your friends, it will be obvious that you need to separate yourself from this peer. Other times, it may not be so clear that a friendship is beginning to cause negative outcomes in your life. Some of the more common reasons that you may need to reconsider a friendship are listed below.

ALCOHOL OR DRUG USE

You do not necessarily need to terminate friendships just because someone is using drugs or alcohol. In fact, being able to speak with your friends about behaviors that are bound to cause them suffering is one of the most valuable things you can do to help your friends. However, dealing with substance abuse in teens (and adults, for that matter) is one of the greatest challenges facing our society, and there may be limits regarding what you can do to help. As with T. J., when your friends who have limited awareness of their substance abuse problems and their actions while intoxicated with alcohol or under the influence of drugs jeopardize your relationships with family members, then it may be time to limit your interactions with them. Besides negative consequences with your family, friends with substance abuse problems are often responsible for disrupting your school, homework, and job or other extracurricular activities. If you have friends showing up where you work while under the influence, it can lead to your losing your job or sometimes facing criminal charges, even if you have never used drugs or alcohol yourself.

CRIME

Friends who get involved in serious criminal activities are likely to jeopardize your future. If you have knowledge of friends who are thinking of committing a crime, you should do your best to encourage them to make a better decision. As with your friends who may have begun to use drugs or alcohol, you can try to be a positive influence and steer your friends to a better path. If, however, you feel concerned for your own safety in speaking with your friends or if you feel that there is nothing you can do to change their decision, then it is in your best interest to end the friendships.

CHEATING

The biggest responsibility for teens is to perform well at school. Teens who do not finish high school are at high risk for many negative outcomes, including drugs, alcohol, jail, unemployment, and increased mental health issues. With increased pressure on teens to obtain solid grades, the temptation to cheat on homework and tests is steadily increasing. Unfortunately, the penalties for getting caught when cheating tend to be severe. You may find yourself in a situation in which one of your friends begins to ask to copy your homework or see your answers on tests. This is a difficult situation for most teens. Even if you do not actively seek answers from someone else, if you knowingly allow others to copy your work you may face the same consequences as your peers. Friends who begin to *repeatedly* focus on finding shortcuts to completing their work, ask other students for answers, and seem to put more effort into cheating than actually studying are likely to lead to future suffering on your part.

Regardless of the reason that you need to end a friendship, it doesn't mean that you automatically need to become enemies with your old friend or even necessarily acknowledge that you have made a decision to spend less time with the person. Depending on the situation, you may need to tell your peer why you no longer are spending as much time talking or hanging out with him or her. It is best to be direct and honest in these situations. For example, you can tell your peer, "Even though you have been a good friend and I like you, I am concerned that you are using marijuana every day and don't feel comfortable being around you as much." Honest statements such as these are better than telling "white lies" to avoid hurting people's feelings. Sometimes these honest statements can help initiate change in your friend's behavior.

HOW TO MAKE NEW FRIENDS

When children are younger, it is easier to make friends. Friendships begin to develop between the ages of three and five. When we are younger, we are not as concerned about what our peers may think about us and tend to act honestly and find friendships with kids that enjoy similar activities. There is a range of "shyness" among people that contributes to our ability to make friends from a young age. At one end of the shyness scale are people who get extremely nervous in social situations. They may experience symptoms such as a rapid heartbeat, sweating and racing thoughts. On the other end of the shyness scale are people with little fear of meeting others. These include kids who have no problem talking to their peers, initiating play activities, or meeting new people. Where you fall on the shyness scale is based on two factors. First, there is a genetic basis to how comfortable you feel in social situations. Just as your height is usually predictable based on your parents height, your shyness is also based on how shy or outgoing your parents are. The second factor is the environment that you are in. If you are in an environment where you have practice meeting new people and have had good experiences from this practice, then this will tend to make you more outgoing. On the other hand, if you have had bad experiences from meeting new people, this will tend to make you more reserved.

By the time you are a teenager, your spot on the shyness scale is well established. The good news is that you can change your spot on the scale. Sometimes, shyness is extreme, and you can actually have a diagnosis called social phobia, which may require more intensive interventions. Usually, however, increasing your awareness regarding your anxieties from meeting new people and developing strategies to improve your social skills can cause dramatic improvements in self-esteem, confidence, and making new friends.

The teenage years tend to be the most frightening time to make new friends but also the time when some of your best lifelong friendships are formed. As the old adage goes, practice makes perfect. This is the good news in making friendships. Every success you have in meeting new people or making new friendships will make it easier the next time around. What is the first step to making new friends as a teen? Depending on your shyness, you may need to practice techniques in making friendships. This includes practicing saying "hello," starting a conversation, or even learning how to invite someone to get together and hang out. Even though it may seem silly, if you can enlist the help of family members or teachers to actually practice these skills, it will make you less fearful when you do it for real.

Besides practicing social skills, you can increase the likelihood of meeting people with shared interests and decrease the stress that comes from making new friends by planning your activities. There are many options for engaging in activities where you can meet people with common interests.

Do You Have Social Phobia?

Do you get anxious in social situations?

Do you get especially nervous when meeting new people?

Are you afraid that you will do something embarrassing whenever you are around your peers?

Do you have physical symptoms from anxiety in social situations? These include fast heartbeat, sweating, rapid breathing, and feeling dizzy or like you are going to faint.

Do your grades (from fear of giving presentations) or activities (from fear of meeting new people) suffer because you are scared of these situations?

If you answered positively to three or more of these questions, then you may have social phobia. See chapter 11 about finding services to get a complete evaluation.

JOINING CLUBS AT SCHOOL

Every high school has a variety of clubs for students, usually run by students with faculty supervision. Your school may have language clubs, a chess club, a computer club, a drama club, and many others. Taking an inventory of what clubs are offered at your school and then picking a club that interests you is a great starting place to meet new people and make new friends.

TAKING COMMUNITY CLASSES

If joining a club is not a good fit for you, exploring different classes offered in your community is another way to meet new people with similar interests. Many cities have a community center that probably offers new classes every six to eight weeks on a variety of topics. These may include cooking, ballroom or hip-hop dancing, martial arts, painting, writing, and others. These classes are sometimes specifically for teenagers and other times may include teens and adults. In addition, local community colleges often have classes at night or on weekends that can fit into your school schedule, increase your social network, and actually help you earn college credit.

TEEN CENTERS

Although it may be scary at first, most cities also have a teen center or at least some designated time in a facility for use by teens. These facilities often have activities such as pool, darts, movies, and Ping-Pong and also arrange a variety of other social events for teens. There is usually some adult supervision, which helps make it a safe environment for teens to interact.

VOLUNTEERING

Volunteering opportunities are present for teens no matter where you live. Some of the more popular volunteer locations for teenagers include libraries, animal shelters, hospitals, and day care centers (helping to take care of younger children). There is always orientation and supervision for volunteer positions, and it is unlikely that you would meet someone who would treat you poorly at one of these locations. Meeting other teens through volunteering is one of the most successful venues for helping shy teens make new friends.

PART-TIME JOB

Depending on your age, you may be old enough to procure part-time employment. Although some jobs can be stressful, you are likely to make many new friends. As adults, the majority of your new friends will come from your workplace, and the skills you can learn as a teen will help you later in life. The money that comes from a part-time job is nice as well. If you do get a job, make sure you strike a balance between work hours and school responsibilities.

WHAT YOU NEED TO KNOW

➤ Perhaps more than anything else, having friends protects you from peer pressure and predicts success for your future.

➤ Having friends who are involved in unhealthy activities can lead to a variety of problems, and thus making good choices in friendships is an important task for you as a teen.

➤ If your friends begin to use poor judgment, don't listen to their advice or let their activities begin to cause problems for you. You may need to end those friendships.

➤ Kids, teens, and adults have varying degrees of shyness, which affects how easy or hard it is to make new friends.

➤ There are ways at school and outside of school that you can meet new people to develop friendships.

5

Are You Being Bullied?

Sonia was a sprightly and confident eighth grader. She belonged to a group of friends consisting of about six girls. Sonia's closest friend from the group was Tracy, with whom she would often hang out separately. One day Sonia was laughing and joking with Tracy during one of their sleepovers. Sonia casually mentioned that one of the other girls from their group, Amelia, was kind of snobby. Being a friend of Amelia's, Sonia thought that her innocent comment was just a harmless part of the fun of recounting memories with Tracy.

The next week, on Monday at recess, Sonia couldn't find her group of friends at the usual spot at which they met. A little puzzled, she started walking around to find them. Far off from their usual spot, Sonia spotted the group and walked over to them. As she smiled to them and waved, one of them saw her, whispered something to a few of the other girls, and led the whole group off. Sonia stood in her spot, aghast, and watched them walk away from her. A leaden weight felt like it dropped into the pit of Sonia's stomach. She felt strangely empty and nauseous at the same time.

A mixture of indignation and confusion ultimately led her to follow them. As she quickened her pace and approached the tail end of the group, they walked away faster and didn't respond to her calls. She stopped in her tracks and finally realized that they were deliberately avoiding her. Sonia was left without a group of friends and went off to eat lunch by herself. In the following weeks, she would occasionally find a lone person to eat lunch with, or she would eat by herself. Later, she learned that her supposedly "faithful" friend Tracy had told Amelia about her meaningless comment. Dangerously full of spite, Amelia was able to engineer the whole group to exclude Sonia.

This form of silent aggression turned out to be extremely painful. Sonia couldn't believe the amount of cruelty these past friends were willing to inflict on her. They saw that she would eat lunch by herself and continued to cut her out, experiencing devilish glee at her bewilderment. Sonia experienced weakness and loss of appetite occasionally. Luckily, she was able to move on to a new school the following year and make a new group of friends, but ultimately she spent the rest of her eighth grade year not belonging.

WHAT EXACTLY IS BULLYING?

Once considered a "normal" part of growing up, being bullied is now both nationally and internationally recognized as damaging to children. The ideas that children should be left to fend for themselves, "toughen up," or "not make a big deal" about being bullied are outdated and dangerous, and we need to work to change our views on this topic. Despite our efforts to educate the public, there are still many caregivers (including school staff and parents) who may refuse to take action to help a child who is being victimized. As adults, in our workplaces there are laws to protect us from harassment, discrimination, and violence. Unfortunately, teenagers are often not afforded these same protections. It should be a universal right that not only are children entitled to an appropriate education but that they be provided a safe environment, free from concerns about being bullied, to promote their learning.

What is the definition of bullying? In general, bullying behavior has three components. First, the bully exhibits behavior directed toward the victim that is designed to hurt, harm, or damage the victim physically, socially, or emotionally. This does not just include direct, overt aggression such as hitting, kicking, or punching (which is more common with boys) but also relational or indirect forms of bullying, such as manipulating and damaging peer relationships through teasing, exclusion, and spreading rumors (which is more common with girls). Second, there must be an imbalance of power when the bullying behavior occurs, with the bully having more power than the victim. Finally, the behavior must happen repeatedly over time to fit the "scientific" definition of bullying. If there are one or two times that you have been harassed but this has not occurred repeatedly and there is not a big "status" difference between you and the other teen, then this does not meet the scientific definition of bullying. However, you may still have mental health or academic repercussions from limited bullying behavior. We know from studies that approximately 30% of teenagers are involved in bullying behavior that fits the above definition. However, the rate of teens with some exposure to bullying is much higher. Between witnessing bullying events and exposure to bullying acts, almost everyone is affected by bullying. Most studies show that the peak of bullying behavior is usually around grade seven or eight, with a steady decline beginning through the rest of the school years.

CONSEQUENCES OF BULLYING

We know that bullying behavior has been observed at extremely young ages, generally accepted as beginning on a serious level in second or third grade, continuing with a peak in the middle school years and a gradual decline as children get older. Studies have shown that children who are victims and bullies in third grade tend to remain victims and bullies throughout their school years and into their adult lives. From a mental health standpoint, being victimized has alarming consequences. To begin with, if you are bullied, you are much more likely to experience headaches, stomachaches, and other physical symptoms than are your peers who are not bullied. Teens who are victimized also perform worse in school. More concerning, bullied teenagers have higher rates of depression, anxiety, and suicidal thoughts. In extreme cases, bullying has been associated with tragic consequences, including completed suicides and violence in school. After it was identified that the Columbine perpetrators had been victimized, the United States Secret Service did a study examining the characteristics of students who had initiated school shootings. The results were published in 2002 reporting that being bullied was a factor in 71 percent of school shootings in the United States.

Bullying is not just an American problem. Multiple studies from around the world demonstrate that secondary school students have similar physical and mental health consequences from being victimized no matter where you live. Bullying rates from other countries are similar or higher than those found in the United States. In addition, bullying in schools is not restricted to only poor schools in rough neighborhoods. From elite private schools to the poorest inner-city schools, bullying knows no boundaries.

THE FOUR TYPES OF PEOPLE FROM A BULLYING PERSPECTIVE

All teenagers fall into one of four groups with respect to bullying behaviors. See where you fit:

VICTIMS

Although no student is immune from being victimized, there are some factors that make you more likely to be a target for bullies. Teens who have few friends and tend to isolate themselves are often easy targets for bullies. Doing poorly in school, not taking care of personal hygiene and grooming, and having poor self-confidence also contribute to being victimized. Teens who tend to be quiet and nonconfrontational also are targets for bullies. In general, bullies target their peers that they feel will not confront them or report them to school administration.

BULLIES

As mentioned above, bullying traits are often present in a child as young as kindergarten age. Pure bullies tend to be feared by their peers and use this fear as a "status symbol" at their schools. Most bullies these days do not use physical means to inflict damage but more often indirect aggression (including spreading rumors, exclusion, and subtle harassment methods that are less likely to be observed by adults). Some research even indicates that these indirect methods of bullying can have far more serious consequences than physical fights. Bullies rarely act alone and try to get other students to support them when they attack others. Many of the bullies' "friends" do not truly want to participate in bullying activity but are usually scared to intervene.

BULLY-VICTIMS

This is the group of students who face the most severe mental health consequences from bullying. Bully-victims are the students who are not only targeted by bullies but also do acts that cause harm to others. Often these students have learned the bullying behavior from being tormented themselves. This can occur when they have an older brother, sister, peers, or even parents who have bullied them. This group of teens does not enjoy the same social standing as the pure bullies and often has few friends, is doing poorly in school, and has a difficult home life.

BYSTANDERS

This is the group that most teens fall into. The bystanders are the teens who are not repeatedly victimized and do not participate in

Are You a Bully or a Victim?

It may not be as easy as you think to decide if you are a bully or are being victimized. Take the quizzes below to get a better idea of where you stand.

1. I have called other students bad names.	YES	NO
2. I have teased other students.	YES	NO
3. I have been intentionally mean to other students.	YES	NO
4. I have pushed or slapped other students.	YES	NO
5. I have hit or kicked other students.	YES	NO
6. I have told other students I will hit or hurt them.	YES	NO
7. I have given other students mean or "dirty" looks.	YES	NO
8. I have said mean things about a student to make other people laugh.	YES	NO
9. I have felt bad because of what I did to another student.	YES	NO
10. I have made other students feel sad on purpose.	YES	NO

If you answered yes to more than three questions above, then you may meet criteria to be classified as a bully.

bullying behavior. Unfortunately, most students in this group usually do not intervene when they witness bullying behavior for fear that the bullies will turn their wrath on them. You can probably remember times when you saw someone else being bullied but were unable or unwilling to assist the person for this reason.

COMMON FORMS OF BULLYING FOR TEENS

Bullying can take many different forms. Many people still think that bullying is when the kid who is a foot taller and a hundred pounds

1. I have been hit or kicked by other students.   YES NO

2. Other students have made me cry.   YES NO

3. Other students have teased me.   YES NO

4. Other students have taken things from me that I did not want to give them.   YES NO

5. Other students have ignored me on purpose.   YES NO

6. Other students have looked at me in a threatening manner.   YES NO

7. Other students have made me feel sad.   YES NO

8. Other students have threatened to hurt me.   YES NO

9. Other students have made fun of me.   YES NO

10. There are days I want to stay home from school to avoid certain students.   YES NO

11. At breaks I often have no one to hang out with.   YES NO

If you answered yes to more than six questions above, then you may meet criteria to be classified as a victim.

heavier than everyone else goes around threatening to beat people up and take their money. This type of bullying does still exist but constitutes only a small amount of bullying behavior. Below are common types of bullying behavior in teens.

DIRECT BULLYING: THREATS AND VIOLENCE

The threat of violence is a more common form of bullying than actual violence. Many bullies maintain their reputations by threatening numerous peers throughout the day. The threats can range from mild to extreme. Threats can be directed at physical harm coming to you ("I'm going to kick your butt after school") or destruction of your property ("The next time I see your bike I'm going to slash your tires"). Threats are the main way bullies try to prevent themselves from getting in trouble. "If you tell the principal then I will really get you!" is a common statement made by bullies.

Physical violence also still occurs in schools. It is rare for fights to take place on the school campus, but some bullies target students and follow them after school or try to arrange times to fight. Peer pressure on the part of the bullies' friends often pushes the bullies to engage in physical contact, with high risk to both the victim and bully but little risk to those who encourage the behavior.

INDIRECT BULLYING: SPREADING RUMORS, EXCLUSION, AND TEASING

A common form of indirect bullying is, especially among girls, spreading rumors—false information. For some bullies, this can be an anonymous way of attacking their victim. The rumors can be mild but usually take the form of vicious, untrue, and demeaning comments that disseminate quickly through the school. You may be horrified when someone that you don't even know comes up to ask you if something they heard about you is true. Common rumors cover topics such as:

> ➤ sexual orientation
> ➤ sexual activity
> ➤ made-up statements that people claim you said
> ➤ attacks on your family
> ➤ false statements regarding who you like or dislike

Exclusion is another type of victimization. Exclusion occurs when a group of peers who you previously hung out with decides to cut you out of the group. It is rare that an entire group decides to attack someone, and usually this type of bullying is spearheaded by one or two individuals who may feel wronged by the victim or are merely being malicious just to see someone suffer. There are few events in your life that can have so profound an impact as losing your group of friends.

Teasing is different than spreading rumors because comments are made directly to the victims and not said "behind their backs." Teasing takes many different forms. Many bullies use teasing with quick retractions to intimidate or harass their victims yet have a quick excuse for their behavior. For example: Alice was a studious, shy 15-year-old sophomore whose parents were recently divorced.

Alice's mother had been a stay-at-home parent, and when her father left, her mom had no income for several months. During this time, Alice was unable to buy new clothes, and several of the girls from one of the popular cliques at her school noticed this. The head of the group, Mary, decided that teasing Alice about her clothes would be a fun thing to do. At the beginning of their English class, Mary would come up to Alice and say things such as "Hey Alice, which used-clothing store did that outfit come from" or "I have some old shirts I was going to throw away but maybe you could use them." Before Alice could even respond, Mary would quickly say "Just kidding" or "You know I'm joking, right?" just as the other students were laughing at her comments. As these comments continued, Alice began to feel increasingly anxious about going to school and began to have physical symptoms (stomachaches and headaches) from the stress.

STEP-BY-STEP APPROACH TO STOP BULLYING

No matter what type of bullying you experience, the procedure for dealing with the situation and putting a stop to it is the same. You can follow the steps below to put an end to bullying. If you are not comfortable tackling some of the steps on your own, it is OK to skip them or ask friends to help you complete them. We will follow-up on some of these themes in the next chapter.

Step one: Make sure you understand all of the behavior that is considered bullying. Many teens feel that if they are not being physically harmed then they are not being bullied and cannot do anything to prevent the behavior from continuing. *This is not true.* As mentioned above, actual physical harm is one of the least common types of bullying that teens experience. Teasing, spreading rumors, exclusion, and threats all are considered bullying behavior. Familiarize yourself with the different types of bullying so you know when you need to act.

Step two: Tell the bully to stop his or her behavior. Depending on your situation, you may not feel that you can do this. It can be anxiety provoking to stand up to a bully. However, looking the perpetrator straight in the eye and telling him or her that you don't like the behavior and to stop often solves the problem quickly. Remember, most bullies will not target people who give them any type of resistance. A serious, direct, honest response to the tormenter regarding the behavior is a strong deterrent to future bullying.

Step three: Start tracking data: When bullies do not respond to simple, direct requests to cease their behavior, it is time to start collecting and recording information on the bullying behavior. You can create your own log of bullying incidents. Mark down the date, time, and place of every episode of harassment. Give as many details as possible, including any bystanders or teens who were encouraging the bullies' behavior. Having this data will be vital in ending the bullying behavior.

Step four: Speak with school personnel. As you begin tracking data, it is also time to speak with school staff. In high school, it is usually best to go directly to the administrative office. Many high schools designate the vice principal or a certain guidance counselor as the contact for harassment issues at school. If you have a good relationship with one of your teachers and the bullying episodes are restricted to one class, then you may be able to speak with a teacher for help. Whomever you decide to speak with, tell them exactly what has been happening, present your data if you have collected any, and gauge their response. If they respond with "This is not a big deal" or "You need to solve your own problems," then you will have to go to someone with more authority. Unfortunately, sometimes the principal of the school will minimize your problem and be of little assistance. This is when you will need to get your parents or another adult advocate involved.

Step five: Tell your parents or another adult outside of school. Even though this is listed at step five, talking to your parents may be the first step you want to pursue if you are being bullied. However, if you are trying to handle the issue on your own and school staff is not responding, then you will need the support of an adult to take the next steps.

Step six: Have your parents contact the school or school district. If the administration at your school has not intervened on your behalf, then your parents need to contact the principal, explain what is happening, and request that the school solve the problem. Proper initial steps by school staff in dealing with bullies include speaking with the bully to inform him or her that the behavior must stop. If it continues, then the school should contact the parents of the bully to enlist their help in ending the behavior. If this fails, then disciplinary measures (such as school suspensions) should begin. If this is not successful, moving the bully to a different school or expulsion is the final step in the process. As the victim, you should never be the student who changes schools unless you desire this. Your parents need to be unrelenting in making repeated contacts with the school, documenting what they are told, and asserting their demands for a safe educational environment. If the school administration is unable to put a stop to the bullying behavior or is unresponsive or slow in its actions, then your parents should contact the district office of the school.

Step seven: Involve the legal system. If staff at the school district office is unable to end the bullying, you may be forced to involve the legal system. This can take two forms. To begin with, harassment, threats, and violence are illegal, and the police can be involved if these events are occurring. Again, having a detailed record of what has transpired is vital information for the police. In addition, civil charges can be brought against the bully and the parents of the bully if they do not stop their behavior. In addition, lawsuits can be brought against school districts for failure to maintain a safe learning environment. The parents of a bully can be sued for defamation, invasion of privacy, and intentional infliction of emotional distress. There are few parents who would not intervene to put an end to their child's bullying behavior if contacted by a lawyer for an impending lawsuit. The resources list at the end of the book lists Web sites that can provide information on bullying laws in each state and legal options available to stop emotional and physical injury. Almost all states have laws against bullying at this time.

Step eight: Seek help for mental health issues if needed. If you begin to suffer symptoms of depression or anxiety, then seek help for these symptoms. Chapter 8 goes into detail about the mental health symptoms you may face when dealing with bullying and the tragic consequences that can occur if you don't get help.

WHAT YOU NEED TO KNOW

> ➤ Bullying consists of repeated acts intended to hurt, harm, or damage the victim physically, socially, or emotionally.
> ➤ Almost everyone is personally affected by bullying or knows someone who is affected by bullying.
> ➤ Bullying is present in all schools regardless of the schools' socioeconomic class.
> ➤ Both bullies and teens who are victimized have an increased rate of mental health problems.
> ➤ Teens fall into four groups with respect to bullying behavior: bullies, victims, bully-victims, and bystanders.

➤ There are two types of bullying behavior, direct and indirect. Direct bullying behavior consists of threats and actual physical violence. Indirect bullying behavior inflicts emotional damage by means such as spreading rumors, exclusion, and teasing.
➤ You can take a step-by-step approach to put a stop to bullying behavior.

6

The Risks and Rewards of Truth Telling

Yessina was a tall and athletic ninth grader. Despite being shy and quiet, she was a star player on the girls' volleyball team and a stellar math student. On a sunny day in March, she went into the cafeteria after a meeting with her volleyball team. A few feet away from her, a boy with glasses suddenly called out "Your nose looks like a horse's nose!" Shocked, Yessina turned around to see the back of the boy's blue baseball cap as he walked away.

A few days after the cafeteria incident, she was standing outside the gym when suddenly she felt a sharp and crumbly substance hit her back. As Yessina heard the taunting exclamation "Horse poop!" she saw dirt falling to the floor beneath her. The same boy with the blue baseball cap ran away behind her. Frozen, Yessina felt her cheeks flush with embarrassment and panic. She couldn't understand why this boy would go out of his way to make her suffer. Filled with indignation and shame, hot tears began rolling down her face.

Two of her friends ran to her, asking, "Yessina, what just happened?" She tearfully explained to them that a boy had taunted her about her nose and thrown dirt at her within a few days. She covered her nose and mouth as she explained this to her friends. Yessina's friends hovered around her and hugged her. The boy came around with a group of his friends and taunted, "Hey, horse nose, I see you're telling your friends! If you tell anybody else, I'll tease you 10 times worse and get my friends to tease your friends. Horse nose, ha ha!" Yessina's silent tears beat down her face furiously as she shrunk away from the mean boy's vision.

Yessina's friends insisted that they inform someone at the school about what was happening. Despite how much she was suffering by the taunting of the boy, Yessina was really worried about the potential consequences of "telling on them." The boy had used a successful and notorious bullying tactic: scaring the victim into thinking it is better to silently take the abuse. However, Yessina was lucky in that her friends made her feel at ease and assured her that she would be better off if they told someone.

Yessina's friends told the principal, and the principal called the boy into her office. The boy got a serious disciplinary lecture and detention. His "threats" of increasing his teasing and of having his friends tease Yessina's friends never materialized. Although the boy never taunted Yessina again, she found herself covering her nose and mouth from time to time because of her memories of this event.

GENERAL COMMUNICATION ISSUES

Communication skills are an essential part of healthy, successful relationships and are linked to positive mental health, academic achievement, career success, and positive self-esteem. Communication skills develop beginning in preschool and are further refined through elementary and middle school. The most growth with respect to communication skills occurs during high school and college. Although your level of shyness can affect your comfort with speaking to other people, even people who are extremely shy can learn to be effective communicators.

There are some basic concepts with regard to communication that you can assess and then work to develop. Depending on the situation, your level of comfort and skill with communication can vary. Take a moment to think about the people you interact with and decide where you have strengths and in which situations you have increased anxiety. You may be very comfortable speaking with your parents or close friends but be intimidated when you need to speak with teachers or peers you don't know. Read the concepts below with regard to communication skills, and see what you can adopt to ease your tension when in difficult situations.

COGNITIVE AWARENESS

Cognition is a term that refers to our thoughts and the processes we go through to achieve understanding. Cognition is affected by our intelligence, perception (what we think is happening), logic (our process of reasoning), and prior experience. There are specific therapy treatments for anxiety that focus on changing our cognitive processes, and these techniques have demonstrated the best results for helping people over-come fears. For teenagers, cognition is in a strong developmental phase. Most teens are not aware of this development, but as your knowledge and experiences increase, so do your cognitive abilities. Taking steps to further focus on your cognitive processes can lead to an increase in communication skills and a decrease in anxiety. Here are some tech-niques you can implement to help improve your cognitive abilities.

"Wait a sec!" When engaged in conversation or presented with a new situation, teens (and adults) often rush to respond, either with their actions or words. The key to stimulating cognitive growth is learning to take a few seconds to thoroughly think about the situation or conversation before responding. In these few seconds, ask yourself a few questions. First, explore what is happening around you. This may include assessing the mood (happy, sad, nervous, angry) of the people around you, assessing what is being asked of you, and thinking of several possible responses and the outcomes they will generate.

Be a good listener. One of the best skills in life you can develop is being a good listener. Perhaps no other skill can help you make friends and succeed academically and in your future career than the ability to listen well. Test yourself to see how well you listen. The next time you are speaking with a friend, family member, or are in class, tell yourself that you are going to focus on everything that is being said. See how well you are able to take in the words and really "hear" what the other person is saying without your mind drifting.

Empathy. Empathy is the ability to recognize the emotions and state of mind of another individual. Empathy is usually lacking in bullies and people who are unable to make friendships. Having empathy improves your communication skills because it allows for greater understanding of what your peer is experiencing. Even when deal-ing with someone who does not demonstrate empathy toward you, if you can maintain empathy for that individual, it will be of benefit in managing the situation.

Respect. Most teens are familiar with the concept of respect. One of the biggest concerns among parents of teenagers is that they do not respect others nor themselves, and this leads to bad things happen-ing. Respect is a key component to communication skills.

Visualization / mental practice. A well-documented technique for improving communication skills is training yourself to practice social situations in your mind. In therapy sessions that teach teens to make new friendships, deal with bullies, or speak to teachers or their parents, I always go through simulations of upcoming events.

Communication Quiz

The source of most conflict among children, teenagers, and adults is poor communication. Problems in communication lead to unreal expectations between teens and their parents, which result in feelings of resentment and unnecessary arguments. Answer the following questions to get an idea of the strength of your communication with your parents.

1. My parents and I eat dinner together most days. YES NO

2. My parents regularly tell me significant events that happen during their days. YES NO

3. My parents are good listeners. YES NO

4. If something bad happens to me, my parents are one of the first people I tell. YES NO

5. If I am stressed out, I can count on my parents to lend me support and help me feel better. YES NO

6. In an emergency, I would call my parents first for help. YES NO

7. My parents regularly ask me how I am doing. YES NO

8. My parents know who most of my friends are. YES NO

9. My parents care about what happens to me in the future and want me to be successful. YES NO

10. I consider my parents to be my friends. YES NO

If more than three of your responses are "No," then your communication with your parents could be improved.

This includes having the teenager think about how the encounter will unfold and explore different ways of handling themselves in the situation. This technique is especially helpful when you have knowledge of an upcoming stressful event.

RELAXATION TRAINING

Even teens who are not shy and have a lot of experience meeting new people or giving presentations may still experience nervousness in social settings. Depending on your personality traits, you may have physical symptoms from being put in social situations or when you know that you will be meeting new people. There are two techniques that you can practice and learn to do without other people noticing that may help you manage these symptoms.

Deep breathing. Deep-breathing relaxation techniques have been practiced for centuries, and the basic method has been constant through this time. We know that the mind is capable of causing multiple physical symptoms in our body. Think about the last time you were nervous about something. You may have noticed that your palms got sweaty, you had a hard time focusing your thoughts, your heart was racing, and you had a hard time catching your breath. In addition, you may have felt stomach upset and gotten a headache. All of these symptoms are real physical symptoms triggered by what is happening in your mind. If you can trigger these symptoms, then it is logical that you can learn to stop the symptoms as well. This is how deep breathing can help. When you begin to feel anxious or nervous, you should practice deep breathing. Accompanied with deep breathing is visualization. Two visualizations you might try are, first, imagining that you are blowing out candles on your birthday cake. You want to get all the candles extinguished on your first breath. Take a deep breath in through your nose, and then in a slow, steady stream release the air from your lungs through your mouth. When blowing out candles, you don't immediately push all the air out of your lungs. Rather, you move from candle to candle in a slow, steady, controlled motion. Second, pretend you are blowing bubbles. Again, you normally want to release as many bubbles as possible when blowing through a bubble wand. You take a deep breath and then use a slow, steady stream of air to generate hundreds of bubbles. Once you have the tempo down, you can shift your visualization during the deep breathing. You should repeat your deep breathing until you begin to notice your heart rate slowing and a feeling of calmness returning to your body. Focus on nothing but your breathing. Let go of the racing thoughts in your mind, and pay attention only to the breath in and out of your lungs. With continued practice, you will be able to significantly decrease your stress level and lower your heat rate, sometimes in as little as one to two minutes.

Progressive muscle relaxation. Progressive muscle relaxation (PMR) is another well-proven method for releasing tension and getting an immediate benefit by decreasing anxiety. Perhaps you have seen "stress balls" for sale at various stores. Stress balls provide "small-scale" muscle relaxation. PMR training involves learning about different muscle groups in your body, choosing a few that are easy for you to contract, and developing a progressive pattern of tightening (flexing) the muscles and then releasing (relaxing) the muscles. Studies have shown that people who practice PMR can often drastically decrease their anxiety and stress levels. Here are the basic steps:

1. Identify muscles that are easy for you flex. One muscle group that tends to work well for almost everyone is your hands. Other muscle groups that are easy to identify can include your bicep, tricep, forearm, abdominal (stomach) muscles, quadriceps, and calf muscles. For each person, there are some muscles that will be easier to flex than others. Although any muscle can be used, it is beneficial to find muscles that you can flex while seated, so that if you need to do PMR while in the classroom, it will not be an obvious distraction to anyone. Identify three muscles that work well for you.
2. After identifying the muscles you want to use, it is time to practice flexing and releasing each muscle. You should start with your hand muscles. Practice squeezing one hand at a time as tight as possible. Putting an object (such as a rubber ball) in your hand and then squeezing the object may make this process easier. Try to keep squeezing your hand for 30 seconds. During this time, pay close attention to the feelings in your hand. Although it should not be painful, there may be a slight discomfort as the blood flow to your hand is restricted and the muscle works to stay flexed. Your hand may feel mildly cold. As you are flexing the muscle, keep your breathing steady, in through your nose and out through your mouth. The key to PMR is to pay attention to the feeling in your muscles when you relax them. After 30 seconds, release your hand. Immediately, the blood flow will return, and you should notice your hand getting warmer. The feeling of relaxation in your hand should

extend up through your arm and shoulder. Focus on this feeling of relaxation. After you have rested for 15 seconds, squeeze both hands again, and repeat the process a total of three times.

3. When you have mastered the process with your hands, do the same thing with the other muscle groups you have identified. The pattern is to tense (squeeze) the muscles for 30 seconds, relax the muscles for 15 seconds, and repeat the process twice more. Breathe in through your nose and out through your mouth in a steady pattern. Focus on the feeling of warmth and relaxation that comes when you release the tension in each muscle and how this feeling can extend through your entire body. The whole process of PMR can be completed in five to 10 minutes and can even be done in a classroom setting without your peers noticing.

CONFRONTING THE BULLY

As mentioned briefly in the previous chapter, the first step in addressing bullying consists of speaking to the bullies themselves. If you are in a situation in which this is just not possible, or if you have tried this already, then you may need to go to the next step. Bullying situations in which there has been actual physical violence or threats with knives, guns, or other weapons require more serious intervention, and multiple people (parents, school personnel, and police) should be notified. Otherwise, even if you have tried speaking with your tormentor in the past, it may be worth learning a few tips for communication and then trying again. Bullies are less likely to continue harassing people once they stand up to them or even challenge what they say. It is almost a guarantee that bullies will continue to target you if you do not respond to their behavior.

To get your point across to the bully, pay attention to the following details.

Posture. No matter your height, you want to stand tall when speaking to bullies. Many teens do not pay attention to their posture. Having poor posture sends a signal that you have poor self-esteem and makes it less likely that people will respect what you say.

Eye contact. How well do you look people in the eye when speaking with them? Although the best time to intervene to improve eye contact is when you are young (ages five to seven), you can change this habit at any time by increasing your awareness and practicing.

You can begin by practicing your eye contact in the mirror and then practice with friends or family members. When you start a conversation with someone or when you are listening, look the person directly in the eyes. Although it may feel strained or uncomfortable at first, soon it will become second nature, and you won't even have to think about it anymore. If you have good eye contact when addressing a bully, it will demonstrate that you are not afraid of him or her and that you will not be a victim.

Be direct. When you are being bullied, the first thought you may have is to wonder why the bully is targeting you. Although you may feel the need to ask "Why are you doing this to me?" or "What did I do to you?" these questions usually do not lead to any resolution of conflict. In fact, these statements can often reinforce the bullying behavior. It is better to hold off on these questions and instead address the behavior that you want to stop. Be honest, direct, and firm. Tell the bully, "What you are doing is wrong and I don't like it. You need to stop directing this behavior at me, or I will be taking steps to protect myself from your harassment." You can be more specific by addressing the actions that the bully is doing (be it spreading rumors, threats of physical violence, etc.). After you make your statement, do not feel the need to justify yourself or explain anything to the bully. Once you have made this direct statement to the bully, there is a good chance that he or she will stop the behavior.

Practice possible scenarios. Nothing works as well as practice for decreasing anxiety about any situation. This includes bullying. Odds are that you know something about the person who is bullying you and thus can think about how he or she will react to your speaking to him or her. Practice out-loud what you plan to say the next time a bullying event occurs. If possible, enlist the help of family or friends to role play the situation. Have your partner pretend to be the bully, and practice different direct, honest statements until you feel comfortable with what you want to say. The more effort you put into practicing, the easier it will be in the real situation.

SPEAKING WITH TEACHERS AND SCHOOL STAFF

Perhaps there is no greater misperception with respect to bullying than that telling someone about what is happening will only make things worse. Bullies will target peers from whom they can get a "fear" response. Once they have received this response, it lets bullies know that they have found a victim and can proceed with their threatening behavior. In order for them to continue their behavior without consequence, often bullies threaten to make your life "even more miserable" if you speak with any school personnel. It is important that these comments not stop you from taking proper steps to bring the bullying behavior to an end. If you have tried communicating with the bully to no avail or if you have real fears for your safety in confronting the bully, then the next step is to speak with school personnel.

In middle schools and high schools, there is usually a dean of students, school counselor, or other staff member identified as the person responsible for handling safety and discipline issues. This can be a good place to start. If you have a teacher who you trust, you may want to speak with him or her about the problem as well. The main thing for you to be aware of is that anyone you speak to who downplays or minimizes your problem is not going to be a good resource for you. Try to identify several people at your school who can be supportive. When speaking with school staff, use the same techniques for communication listed above. Tell him or her you need to speak with him or her about harassment that you are enduring at school. Stand up straight, make good eye contact, and be direct and firm in reporting what is happening. If you have been taking notes on the bullying episodes, you should show them.

Different schools will handle bullying in different ways. Many schools are adopting a no-tolerance policy on bullying, and if your school has one, you should review it before speaking with school personnel (mainly so you can remind them of what is written in the policy). A reasonable first step for school administration is to speak with the bully. They may ask to meet together with you and the perpetrator. If you are uncomfortable with this, then you need to express this to school personnel. You should not be forced into this meeting. We would not ask an adult to sit down with someone who has been threatening them, and the same should apply to teens. If, however, you feel that having school personnel present for a meeting with the bully may lead to a quick end to the problem, then it is reasonable to attend a joint meeting. At this meeting, the school administrator should identify specifically what behavior has been occurring, why the behavior is not acceptable, and what consequences the bully will face if the behavior continues. These consequences should be presented in written form, and the school staff, bully, and you should sign the form; everyone should receive a copy. This last step is extremely important if the bullying behavior continues or if the school fails in its responsibility to provide you with a safe environment.

After this meeting, if the behavior continues, it is vital that you continue to report any bullying that occurs. In addition to reporting the behavior, document the date that you tell school personnel that the behavior is continuing and the response that you receive. If you feel that you have completed these tasks and have not received proper assistance from your school, then you will need to contact the school district office. This is likely too large a task to pursue on your own, and it is best to enlist the help of your parents or another adult.

HOW TO SPEAK WITH YOUR PARENTS OR CAREGIVER

Unfortunately, many parents are unaware of problems that their children encounter. This includes problems with bullying, friends, academics and even more serious issues such as anxiety or depression. Even when teens are feeling suicidal, their parents often have no idea of the suffering their child is enduring. Part of the natural progression as you age is that you begin to rely less on your parents or other caregivers for support and more on your friends. Parents usually are respectful of this fact and give teens privacy. The problem occurs when you and your parents no longer communicate enough that you feel comfortable asking for help. When it comes to bullying, there are extra barriers to communication with your parents.

Perhaps the number one reason that teens do not want to discuss bullying or other problems at school with their parents is embarrassment and anxiety regarding their parents' response. You are becoming more and more independent as a teenager, and along with this independence comes the idea of solving problems on your own. For most issues, you can get good advice from friends who have dealt with similar problems. However, your peers are unlikely to have the expertise to assist with issues regarding bullying and dealing with school administration. Because of this, you will need to turn to your parents for help. Although the vast majority of parents respond to these requests with empathy and compassion, many teens fear that their parents will think they are weak, immature, or making a "big deal out of nothing." For this reason, you should prepare yourself for the conversation with your parents.

Step 1: Tell your parents or caregiver that there is a serious issue that you need their help with and would like to schedule a time to speak. By doing this, rather than immediately stating "I'm being bullied and I need your help," you are establishing that this is a serious issue that needs their full attention. Many adults have a hard time paying full attention without warning. They may be preoccupied with other thoughts or activities when you initially approach. By scheduling a time to speak, you can be sure to receive their complete attention. Try to schedule a time for later that same day.

Step 2: Sit down when speaking with your parents. It is more effective when communicating with any individual to be seated when speaking. You can use a table, sofa, or any other appropriate seating arrangement.

Step 3: Pay attention to your eye contact and posture. By sitting up straight and not looking down or away, you will emphasize the importance of the discussion to your parents.

Step 4: If your parents tend to interrupt, ask them to just listen. A trait of many caregivers is that they tend to interrupt teens or children rather than let them finish. Caregivers want to immediately offer advice to "fix" the situation. When adults interrupt, it usually leads to teens cutting their story short and not being able to share everything. Even if your parents are good listeners, it is probably a good idea to tell them that you would like to tell them your whole story before they interrupt or ask questions. Adults will respond well to this information, and it will aid them in paying careful attention to what you are saying.

Step 5: When it is their turn to speak, give them respect, listen to what they say without interrupting, and answer the questions they have.

Step 6: Put together a plan of action with your parents. You can show them this book, including the steps outlined in chapter 5, to decide what should happen next.

In the worst-case scenario, if your parents or caregiver are unable or unwilling to help, then you will need to identify another adult who can provide assistance. You probably have other family members (such as an older brother or sister, an aunt, or an uncle) or adult friends (either family friends or neighbors) who can step in to provide assistance.

DEALING WITH FAMILY BULLYING

There is a good chance that bullies at school have been victimized themselves. Often, there may be an older sibling or even a parent who has either knowingly or unknowingly bullied a family member. Teens who have been bullied at home often target peers at school, and this leads to a vicious cycle of violent behavior.

If you are being bullied at home and it is by a sibling, then the first recommended action is to speak with your parents. Use the same steps listed above to let them know what is happening and that the behavior must stop.

If your parents are not able to assist you in dealing with family bullying or if they are abusing you, then you will need to pursue different options. The best choice is to find an adult friend or other family member who can provide assistance. It is scary to think that you may need to report your parents' behavior, but you face far greater health consequences if you remain in a situation in which you are being abused. If you cannot identify an adult who can help you, you may need to call child protective services to be removed from your dangerous home environment and placed in a safe living situation. Calling child protective services does not mean that you will never see your parents again. In fact, child protective services will usually work with families to provide extra support or services to help correct whatever problem is occurring, which can make the home environment much better than it has been in the past.

WHAT YOU NEED TO KNOW

▸ Communication skills are vital not only for your success in life but also for ending victimization.
▸ By increasing your cognitive awareness of your surroundings, you can improve your communication and listening skills.
▸ Speaking to people is an anxiety-provoking situation made worse when you have to address difficult topics such as bullying and victimization.
▸ Deep breathing and progressive muscle relaxation (PMR) are two well-proven techniques to quickly decrease anxiety.
▸ Confronting bullies in a firm, direct manner can often end your problems with the individuals.
▸ If speaking to the bully fails or if you are unable to confront the bully, then you should speak with staff at your school.
▸ The more you practice different scenarios, the more comfortable you will be in the real situation.
▸ Enlisting the help of your parents can be scary, but they almost always provide needed support.
▸ If you are in an abusive situation at home, you may need to call child protective services for help.

7

When Things Get Overwhelming: Mental Health Problems

Kyle attended Cypress Academy, an elite private high school for the children of professors of the local university. His father, a university professor of law, sent him to that school because of its excellent academic reputation. Kyle was half-Asian, but most of the other students at his school were caucasian. Despite this difference, Kyle was one of the most popular guys at school. Friendly and talkative by nature, he had a knack for drawing other kids into his stories. He was well liked and admired by his large group of friends.

In the middle of seventh grade, a new boy named Lucas joined the school. Lucas's father had just been appointed an associate professor of biology at the university. Kyle immediately decided to befriend Lucas in order to help him assimilate into the school and form friends. Kyle invited Lucas to his house and made a special effort to educate him about the different traditions at school. Because of this, Lucas began to successfully assimilate into Kyle's group at school.

A few weeks after Lucas's introduction to his group, Kyle began to have an uncanny feeling that rumors were being spread about him. When he approached his group of friends during recess, they would quietly slink away. Puzzled, Kyle would follow them, and to his dismay, they would run away from him. When Kyle could manage to find them and pretend everything was OK, they would diss him and say mean things. His friends, or maybe ex-friends, said things like "You're a skinny wimp!" and "Hey, look at the loser following us, hahahaha!"

These old friends started to do pranks on his family. They would call Kyle's house and then hang up. One afternoon, as Kyle was returning home from school, he saw that his house had been TP'd—covered all over with toilet paper. Another day a few weeks later, he came home to a scene of scattered plastic cups and shredded paper plates on his lawn. With both the TP and cluttered lawn situations, he had to clean up before his parents got home. During this trying time, his parents had no idea that his friends had turned on him. Kyle's parents had no idea about the agony he was going through—that he felt nausea in the pit of his stomach at the thought of going to school.

The extreme incidents continued. One day they tried to set him on fire. Another day the group "ambushed" him after school, running at him like fighter jets. Yet another day they surrounded him and blasted cold water on his back from a fire extinguisher. He felt himself freezing in shock and ran away through a gap in the boys. This was how his seventh and eighth grade years were spent. The violent abuse horrified him and left an indelible mark on his school experience.

By the ninth grade, Kyle began to skip school entirely. His parents had no idea that he was doing this because he would leave the house in the morning, only to roam around aimlessly in the parks and the library. Kyle was in total despair and too scared to know to whom to turn.

At the end of the ninth grade, Kyle's parents finally discovered the truth. In anger, they called the school principal. Unfortunately, this only served to aggravate the school administration toward the whole situation. The principal and assistant principal blamed Kyle as much as the group of boys for the mess. They reproached Kyle for not speaking up. Of course, they had no idea the pressure that Kyle faced—the pressure to be cool or be defamed as a "wimp." With superficial amendments made and Lucas gone from the school, Kyle resumed school at Cypress Academy in the 10th grade. However, it turned out that the repercussions of skipping most of ninth grade were dire. He was so academically incompetent that he was not deemed qualified to be a 10th grader. Kyle was forced to repeat ninth grade with a cohort of students a year younger than him.

However, even worse than the academic consequences were the consequences to his well-being. Kyle fell into a severe depression. He felt suicidal and lost all concentration for his schoolwork. He would come home from school every day and sulk on the floor of his bedroom. Kyle lost weight and began to become tearful at odd times of the day. Only after a talk with his parents and a subsequent move to a new school was recovery even a viable option. After seeking professional help for treatment, Kyle finally began on the path toward feeling like himself again.

One reason you may be reading this book is because you have been or are being bullied, are bullying others, or are having a hard time dealing with peer pressure and are now experiencing various symptoms that are making it hard to function. As a general rule, the primary "job" for teenagers is to be successful at school. This means functioning well in the classroom and with your peers at school and being able to complete expected homework assignments. In addition, we like to see teens involved in some extracurricular activities. This could include sports, clubs, volunteering, or working at a part-time job. If you are having difficulties with any of these activities, then it is worth exploring what can be done to help you gain success. If, in addition to problems in these areas, you are having other physical or mental health symptoms, then it is necessary to seek professional help.

RISK FACTORS FOR MENTAL HEALTH PROBLEMS

Mental illnesses are diseases that can be caused or influenced by a variety of things. As with most illnesses, part of your risk for mental illness is genetic, and part of the risk comes from environmental factors.

GENETIC RISK

Your genetic risk for mental health problems is something that you cannot change. We know from research into depression, anxiety, and other mental illnesses that certain people are born with a higher risk for illness than others. How do we know this? There are studies done with family members that compare rates of mental health problems. We know from these studies that if your mother, father, or a sibling (brother or sister) has had problems with depression or anxiety, then you are at a higher risk for these problems. If more than one family member has had problems, then your risk is even higher. Think about various family members and whether they have had problems with mental illness. You may want to ask your mother or father to think back to their teenage years and ask them if they were ever depressed or anxious growing up. Knowing about your genetic risk can help you make the decision to seek professional services as needed.

ENVIRONMENTAL RISK

Your environmental risk for developing mental health problems refers to everything that is happening in your life and is something that you can change. There are three main issues that affect your environmental risk. They are home, school, and peers.

HOME
Probably the main environmental risk factor for developing mental health problems is your home. Are you in a supportive environment at home, or are there problems that make your home an unsafe environment? Examples of more minor home issues include poor communication with your parents or other family members. In addition, extreme levels of conflict with siblings can contribute to a poor home environment. More extreme home situations include:

➤ Experiencing verbal, physical, or emotional abuse
➤ Witnessing acts of domestic violence (seeing one parent physically or emotionally abuse the other)
➤ Having a parent or caregiver who is struggling with alcohol or drug addiction
➤ Not having basic needs met. This includes food, clothing, proper heat, and having at least some designated space for yourself (privacy).

If any of these situations are occurring at home, then you are at very high risk for developing mental health problems (including drug and alcohol abuse) and should immediately seek assistance.

SCHOOL
Teens spend a large amount of their time at school. Because of this, if your school is a source of significant stress or harm, then you are at greater risk for mental health problems. Schools can be a poor fit for a number of reasons. Some of the most common problems with school situations include:

Bullying. Any situation involving bullying at school will increase your risk for depression and anxiety.

Lack of friends. This is most often true in small school settings. Although smaller schools can offer advantages, the biggest concern for teens comes from the fact that with a lower number of students, you have a smaller pool of people with whom to become friends. This leaves some teenagers isolated, or on the "outside" of the primary social circle. When you are at a larger school, you are much more likely to find a group of students with similar interests who can become your friends.

How to Tell Whether You May Need Professional Help

If you find yourself experiencing any of the following, you may want to contact a mental health professional.

- ➤ Changes in sleep
- ➤ Loss of interest in doing things you used to enjoy
- ➤ Easily irritable or quick to anger most of the time
- ➤ Frequent suicidal thoughts
- ➤ Stomachaches and headaches related to attending school
- ➤ Significant weight gain or weight loss without trying
- ➤ Crying spells for no clear reason

Academic issues. The traditional classroom setting is not always the best way to learn. Although there is beginning to be more flexibility in approaches to education, the majority of schools still function the same way they did 100 years ago—with lecture-style learning that requires you to sit still and focus for most of the day. For some teenagers, this traditional classroom format leads to poor learning, poor grades, and behavioral issues. Most high schools have alternative educational programs, including independent study (in which you work independently on assignments, sometimes meeting once or twice per week with a tutor or mentor) and "middle" college (in which you enroll in a community college setting, complete your high school coursework, but also begin to accrue college credits). Occasionally, making a change to your educational environment can drastically improve your mental health.

DEPRESSION

Depression is one of the most common medical problems in the United States and throughout the world. Some studies report that depression is the most common reason people go to see their doctor and is responsible for high rates of morbidity (suffering) throughout the world. Teenagers have the same or higher rates of depression as do adults. Adding bullying, victimization, and peer pressure concerns further increases the rate of depression among teens. Data suggest that as many as 50 percent of teens who bully or are bullied may meet the criteria for depression.

There is a difference in feelings of sadness that most teenagers experience and in clinical depression. How can you know if your depression warrants professional help?

TIME

How long do you have feelings of depression? If you feel depressed for part of a day or even for one to two days but then the feelings of depression go away and you no longer feel down, then this is likely not clinical depression. However, if you look back over the past two weeks and feel that for the majority of days you have been depressed, then this is likely clinical depression.

SUICIDAL THOUGHTS

It is a normal part of teenage development to occasionally have some thoughts regarding what it would be like if you were dead. If these thoughts begin to consume a significant amount of time (for example, occurring daily, every other day, or several times per week), then they can be symptoms of depression.

APPETITE AND SLEEP

If you begin to have changes in either your sleep or appetite, they may be attributed to depression. The changes can go either way. For example, if you are no longer hungry and find yourself not interested in eating and begin to lose weight without trying, these are causes for concern. In addition, if you find that you are hungry all the time and begin to gain weight, this can also be a symptom of depression. Similar to appetite, problems with sleep are very common in depression. If you feel tired all the time, find yourself increasing the length of time you sleep at night, and begin to take naps during the day, this may be due to depression. Other sleep problems associated with depression include having problems falling asleep, being unable to "turn off your mind," or waking up repeatedly during the night.

IRRITABILITY, ANGER, AND GUILT

Although many parents and caregivers are able to recognize these symptoms in teens, they often don't attribute them to depression.

By the time you are a teenager, you are probably aware of your nature with respect to how quick you get irritated with your family or peers. If you begin to notice that you lose your patience quickly and are increasingly frustrated with your parents or friends, then this is a warning sign. Guilty feelings are also a symptom of depression. Feeling bad about your actions at school or home, even when they have not caused any serious harm, is a very common sign of depression.

LOSING INTEREST IN FRIENDS OR ACTIVITIES
Many teens have a wide variety of interests. This may include watching TV, caring for a pet, playing computer games, speaking on the phone, or hanging out with friends. Any sudden change in your desire to do any of the activities you enjoy is likely a symptom of depression. Also, a symptom of depression is if you "force" yourself to continue with your usual activities but no longer take the enjoyment from them that you had in the past.

POOR CONCENTRATION OR AGITATION
Most teenagers spend a lot of time in a structured classroom setting. You may be taking five to seven classes that require you to pay attention. Because of this, it will probably be easy for you to tell if you are having problems focusing on what is being said. If you begin to daydream frequently or drift off in class, catching yourself after 10 to 20 minutes and not remembering what the teacher has said, then your concentration is negatively affected. If you formally were able to sit at your desk without problems but now find yourself feeling jittery or agitated and feel the need to stand up or get out of your seat frequently, then this is a cause for concern.

ANXIETY

Anxiety disorders are the most common psychiatric disorders in teenagers and children. As many as one in five teenagers may meet criteria for a clinical anxiety disorder. There are several different anxiety disorders, and the odds of having any of them increase when bullying or victimization are involved.

GENERALIZED ANXIETY DISORDER (GAD)
The main feature of generalized anxiety disorder is worrying about multiple future events. When these worrying thoughts begin to occur on a daily or constant basis, then you may have GAD. Usually, people with GAD have a hard time focusing on day-to-day tasks and appear

Comments to Initiate Conversation Regarding Bullying or Mental Health

"It seems like you are having some problems with bullying."

"You seem sad lately—what's going on?"

"How can I help you?"

"Tell me what is going on."

"You seem really down lately. Do you want to talk about it?"

What *Not* to Say:

"Don't be such a wimp."

"Just fight them."

"Don't tell anyone or it will get worse."

preoccupied and distracted throughout the day. For teens it may be especially difficult to focus in the classroom setting.

SOCIAL PHOBIA

The main feature of social phobia is experiencing feelings of nervousness associated with upcoming events that occur in a social setting. For teens with social phobia, even making it to school each day can cause considerable anxiety. People with social phobia are usually concerned that something they say or do will bring ridicule to them, which makes them feel even more anxious. Your fear of doing something embarrassing may lead you to cut classes or find ways to skip school to avoid social situations.

PANIC DISORDER

Panic disorder is when you have experienced a panic attack and spend time worrying that you will have another panic attack. Panic attacks are sometimes associated with social phobia and other anxiety disorders as well. A panic attack is when you have the rapid onset of several physical symptoms, usually reaching a peak in 10 minutes. The symptoms are due to anxiety and can include a rapid heartbeat, sweating, nausea, shaking, dizziness, and having a feeling of "losing control" or "going crazy."

OBSESSIVE-COMPULSIVE DISORDER (OCD)

Obsessive-compulsive disorder is when you either have intrusive thoughts that cause you distress or you feel you must perform certain behaviors (for example, washing your hands, touching an item an exact amount of times, or always smiling at people you don't know) in order to prevent something bad from happening. Often, the "bad" thing is something that may seem irrational (like your parents will die if you don't touch the doorknob three times on the way out of your house each morning) when you stop and think about it, but nevertheless you cannot control your fears.

POST-TRAUMATIC STRESS DISORDER (PTSD)

Post-traumatic stress disorder is an anxiety disorder that people develop after being exposed to a traumatic event. The event may have happened directly to you, or you may have witnessed the event occur to someone else. A "traumatic" event can be different from person to person but usually involves the risk of severe harm or some type of life-threatening event. Bullying episodes can lead to symptoms of PTSD. The most common symptoms include unpleasant, recurrent dreams or memories of the events and an association with heightened anxiety responses. Some examples of the anxiety symptoms include being extremely jumpy and "on edge," or nervous, all the time. People usually try to avoid doing things that remind them of the trauma.

TREATMENT

For all mental health issues, there are several types of interventions: social, psychotherapeutic, and biological (exercise and medication).

SOCIAL INTERVENTIONS

Social interventions are changes that can happen at either your home or school to help alleviate symptoms of depression or anxiety. Home interventions usually address how well various family members are getting along. When meeting a new client, therapists should always ask about how things are going at home and whether you are aware of any problems with your parents (or other caregivers in the house). They should ask about the level of stress in the house. Are there financial problems? Are your parents fighting, and are you concerned that they may be getting a divorce? Is there any drug or alcohol abuse occurring regularly in your home? By doing a proper assessment of your social environment and addressing glaring problems, you will almost definitely see an immediate improvement in your mental health.

PSYCHOTHERAPEUTIC INTERVENTIONS

The next type of intervention to address mental health issues is psychotherapy. Even though there are more than 300 types of therapy, there are two specific types that have been best studied in teenagers and have demonstrated the most efficacy. These are cognitive-behavioral therapy (CBT), which works to treat depression and anxiety, and interpersonal psychotherapy (IPT), which is used to treat depression. These treatments are considered evidence-based medicine. *Evidence-based medicine* refers to the practice of medicine (including not only mental health but the practice of all medicine) that is based on the results of scientific evidence. Thus, even though there are hundreds of therapy treatments, the two that are considered the best evidence-based treatments are CBT and IPT. These therapy techniques have been studied in well-designed research and have specific protocols and success rates for treating teenagers. If you decide to participate in psychotherapy, it is important for you and your parents to ask specific questions regarding therapy treatment. Historically, some people have not understood what happens in the psychiatrist's or therapist's office. Mental health treatment should be the same as any other medical treatment. There should be no "mystery" about what happens during therapy treatment. Your therapist should be able to describe the therapy process, explain exactly what is going to take place, and tell you projected success rates. There should also be goals and time limits set for an initial evaluation of how well the treatment is working, typically three months. A usual treatment course for psychotherapy for patients consists of:

1. A comprehensive interview with both the teenager and parents
2. The completion of some mental health symptoms rating scales. Although these are not absolutely diagnostic, they can provide a good baseline rating for the severity of your current symptoms of depression or anxiety.
3. An in-depth discussion regarding therapy treatment
4. When therapy commences, the first few sessions consist of the "trust-building" phase. Research has shown that if you do not have a good rapport with your therapist within the

first few sessions, then your treatment is less likely to be successful.
5. Most psychotherapy treatments should initially last about 20 weeks.
6. If, after 20 weeks, your therapy is not yielding benefits to your mental health symptoms, then you may need to reevaluate your treatment.

Cognitive-behavioral therapy. Probably the best-studied therapy treatment for helping children, teenagers, and adults is cognitive-behavioral therapy (CBT). One of the theories behind cognitive-behavioral therapy is that our mood state is determined by our thoughts and behaviors in response to our environment. Teenagers who are greatly affected by events outside their control and are motivated to feel better are a good fit for this type of treatment. You can explore whether CBT may be beneficial for you by asking yourself some simple questions.

1. Am I willing to meet with someone every week and share my thoughts and feelings about important events in my life? It is not expected that you immediately need to share your innermost secrets or personal beliefs. However, after developing some trust and comfort with your therapist, the responsibility to bring problems to the sessions is yours. If, after four to six sessions, you do not feel comfortable with your therapist, then you should change therapists. We know from research that no matter how competent your therapist may be, if you do not feel comfortable with him or her, then it is highly unlikely that your treatment will be successful.
2. Am I willing to complete brief assignments outside my therapy sessions? These assignments usually involve keeping a thought and/or feeling record, challenging yourself to do some activities you may feel uncomfortable with, or taking notes on conflicts and stressful situations that occur during the week.
3. Am I willing to challenge my way of thinking about situations and life? This involves being open to new ideas and being optimistic that changing current thinking patterns can lead to improvements in your mood or anxiety levels. For many teens, this can be a difficult process, and if CBT fails to lead to improvement, this is the most likely cause. Ask yourself how you respond to people who challenge some of the things you say or do. Are you a very defensive

person? Do you feel personally attacked or degraded if someone wants you to explore other ways of accomplishing tasks or solving problems? If you can be flexible in these situations, then CBT will be a good treatment option.

Interpersonal psychotherapy. Interpersonal psychotherapy uses some of the techniques of CBT but focuses on problems in your relationships. It seeks to mend them, thereby leading to a resolution of depressive symptoms. Interpersonal psychotherapy is not a treatment for anxiety disorders, though anxiety and depressive symptoms tend to occur together, so there may be some benefit to IPT in alleviating anxiety. If you find that you and your parents or other caregivers are constantly arguing or if you feel anxious about speaking with your parents over trivial matters, then IPT may help solve these issues. IPT is also a viable treatment if you tend to have problems in your peer relationships, including making and keeping friends, and find that you tend to get into fights or arguments with your peers. As with CBT, you need to have a willingness to share events from your life and challenge yourself to make changes in how you interact with peers.

EXERCISE

Exercise has long been known to decrease your risk of medical problems. Exercise leads to benefits that include preventing obesity, lowering cholesterol levels, lowering blood pressure, keeping your immune system healthy and more able to fight off disease, and many others. In addition, regular exercise is associated with improvements in self-esteem and improved academic performance in teenagers. Better than perhaps all of these benefits, however, is that exercise is now recognized as a successful treatment for depressive and anxiety disorders. You have probably heard of endorphins, which are the chemicals that our bodies naturally produce that have positive mood effects (as well as the ability to decrease pain). Endorphins and other neurochemicals that we produce with regular exercise may play a role in the protective effect of exercise on mental health. More information on some simple ways to begin an exercise program are listed in chapter 9.

MEDICATIONS

Sometimes your social situation may be fine, you are not a good candidate for therapy treatment, and you are unable to begin a regular exercise program. If this is the case, then you may be a candidate for pharmacotherapy—using medications to help with your depressive or anxiety symptoms. For some teenagers, medications are the most successful treatment for mental health problems. Some of the more common reasons why medications may be a good treatment for you include:

> ▸ Financial issues: Both weekly therapy and joining a gym or starting an exercise plan can be costly. If your family has limited financial means, then this may be a barrier to certain treatments.
> ▸ Motivation: If you are so depressed that you cannot handle the idea of beginning a regular exercise plan
> ▸ Ability to share thoughts and feelings: Many teens and adults have difficulties with sharing personal issues with others. If the idea of sitting in a therapy office and having someone give you undivided attention to hear about your life frightens you, then therapy may not be the best choice for you. No individual therapy will be successful if you are not motivated to participate in the treatment.

If you are interested in trying medications to help with your symptoms, you should be aware of some information before deciding if medications are a proper treatment, including the following.

Reliability. Can you take a pill each day without forgetting? A large percentage of adults and teenagers (perhaps as many as 50 percent) have problems with proper medication compliance. Assess how well you can remember to do daily tasks or if you can enlist someone else in your household to assist you.

The three-month commitment. Understand that the medications usually take some time to begin working. Although there are teenagers who swear they feel better the day they start taking medications, we know that the benefit from medications may take up to three months to develop. This has led to many teens (and adults) trying medicines for anxiety or depression, taking them daily for two weeks, then not feeling any better, so they stop treatment. Many times, if you continue a medication for the full three months, you will benefit from the treatment. Thus, whenever you make the decision to try medicine, you should tell yourself that you are committing to taking a pill daily for three months before deciding whether to stop treatment or switch to a new medicine.

Dosing. Another issue related to the success rate of medications concerns proper dosing. The philosophy for using medications in teens is best implemented via the concept "start low and go slow."

This means that we start with a low dose of medicine (to help decrease side effects) and make slow increases in the dose. These dose increases should occur during the three month trial. Another common reason medicines fail is because they are not increased to the proper dose. Depending on your choice of medicine, make sure you research and speak with your doctor about the dosing range of the medicine you are taking.

Side effects. Although the most common medicines used to treat anxiety and depression in teens tend to be very well tolerated, you should be aware of some potential side effects. A complete discussion of medication side effects is outside the scope of this book. The important point you can take away is to discuss the side effects in detail with your doctor and read about the medicine from as many sources as possible. A good strategy is to research information on the medication on the Internet and then bring your questions to your doctor.

The myth of personality change. Many teens and their parents are afraid that psychiatric medications will change their personality or cause them to be "zombies." This is not true. There are some psychiatric medications used to treat severe mental illnesses such as schizophrenia that can have side effects that cause sedation (feeling tired), but this is not the usual case with medicines to treat anxiety or depression. Consider how you felt when you were not depressed or anxious (even if it was only for one morning or afternoon). The medication should return you to a mental state similar to when you felt "normal." When you are depressed or anxious, little things that happen during the day tend to cause big emotional reactions—anger, stress, sadness, hopelessness. With medication or any successful treatment, these little things will no longer cause such big negative reactions, you will feel better about yourself and your future, but your core personality and all of your positive traits will stay the same.

Length of medication treatment. Some teenagers are resistant to starting medication because they are afraid they will need to continue with medication for the rest of their lives. This is usually not the case. If you start medication for anxiety or depression and the medication is effective, we know that you have a better chance of not needing to take medicines in the future if you continue for at least one year. Sometimes this is difficult. You may think "I feel fine, I don't need the medicine any longer" and then stop prematurely, only to have your symptoms return. If you are thinking of stopping a medication, let your care provider know. As a teenager, no one can force you to take medication or undergo any other treatment. It is important that you be well informed about the expectations from treatment to give you the best chance for a cure so as not to need treatment at a later time.

DIFFERENT PROFESSIONALS WHO CAN HELP

There are many different professionals who can provide assistance when you are suffering from mental health problems. In fact, one good trend that is occurring in the United States is that with the decrease in stigma regarding mental illness, one of the top employment prospects is working in the health care industry as a mental health professional. Below are some of the types of people who can provide assistance.

SCHOOL COUNSELOR

A logical first choice for many teens, middle school and high school counselors usually have resources to provide assistance for the students at their school. Depending on your school district, you may even be able to receive weekly therapy sessions at your school. Some schools have their own therapists who work with students, and others have someone available who splits his or her time between two or more locations. Even if your school is unable to offer more than brief counseling sessions, your school counselor should be able to assist you with getting connected to services that can provide help.

PSYCHIATRISTS

A psychiatrist is a physician who specializes in the treatment of mental illness. A psychiatrist has completed training at medical school (M.D. degree) and then spent three or four years in additional residency training as a general psychiatrist (many working with adults but some with adolescents and children as well). Then, often psychiatrists who work with teenagers will do an additional two-year fellowship working exclusively with teenagers and children. A child psychiatrist has training in the use of therapy treatments and biological treatments (including medications) and is the best option for treatment if you feel that you may be interested in medications as well as or instead of therapy. Unfortunately, there is a shortage of child and adolescent psychiatrists in the United States, and sometimes it takes several weeks to be seen.

PRIMARY CARE DOCTORS (PEDIATRICIAN AND FAMILY PRACTITIONER)

Pediatricians and family practitioners are physicians who have completed a three-year residency working with adolescents and children (pediatricians) or children, adolescents, and adults (family practitioners). Although there are varying degrees of training that these physicians receive regarding mental health issues, these doctors are often a good first choice for speaking to a professional. Usually you can get in to see your primary care doctor quickly, and they may have referral sources for mental health professionals. Some statistics support the idea that as many as one out of every two or three non–well child (checkup) appointments are in part due to mental health concerns. Because of this, primary care doctors who work with teenagers are usually very experienced in addressing and discussing topics such as anxiety and depression.

PSYCHOLOGISTS

A psychologist is a mental health professional who has usually completed a four- to five-year post graduate (after college) educational program and then additional clinical training (postdoctoral internship) working with patients with mental health issues. Psychologists either have a doctor of philosophy (Ph.D.) or doctor of psychology (Psy.D.) degree. Psychologists who want to work with teenagers will focus on this age group during their training. Psychologists can provide therapy treatments as well as psychological testing. Psychological testing can assess IQ and is helpful for diagnosing issues such as learning disabilities. Psychologists perform mental health assessments and recommend (and perform) psychotherapy treatments for your symptoms.

MARRIAGE AND FAMILY THERAPISTS AND SOCIAL WORKERS

Marriage and family therapists and social workers are therapists who have usually completed a one- to two-year postgraduate program learning about counseling and have also completed an internship working with patients. As with psychologists, these providers may decide to specialize in working with children and families, and if this is the case, most of their internship hours will be with this population. These therapists can provide therapy treatments, and although their training is not as intensive as that of a psychologist or psychiatrist, they are a good option for treatment. Often it may be faster to get an appointment with them, because there are more of them available.

SUICIDAL OR HOMICIDAL THOUGHTS

Suicidal and homicidal thoughts deserve their own special category. In the practice of child psychiatry, the number one goal is to prevent children and teenagers from taking their own lives or the lives of others. Unfortunately, homicide (#2) and suicide (#3) are the leading causes of death for 15 to 19 year olds after accidents. Even though most homicides may not be influenced by mental health issues, certainly every suicide in a teenager is preventable. After several high-profile school shootings (the most famous being Columbine in Colorado in 1999), the United States Secret Service did a study of the characteristics of the shooters. They found that 71 percent of the perpetrators in school shootings had a history of being victimized.

There are many reasons why suicide remains one of the top causes of death for teens. Despite some recent advances in public awareness, there is still a stigma attached to mental illness that may make you hesitant to tell people that you are suffering. You may have told your parents or another adult that you were feeling depressed, and they may have minimized your concerns. It is common for caregivers to tell teens that they will "snap out of it" or "everyone feels depressed sometimes, you'll get over it" and not take the time to actually sit down with you, ask about the depression, and come up with a plan for help. It is hard enough to even bring up the topic of being depressed or anxious, and then when your concerns are not taken seriously, it is less likely that you will bring them up again.

When you find that you are constantly thinking about suicide, that you begin to do Internet searches on suicide, or are actually researching different techniques people use to kill themselves, it is time to get help. As mentioned earlier, having occasional thoughts of what it would be like if you were not alive is normal for teens. However, if you begin to have these thoughts more often than once every few weeks or you find that you have left the "thought" phase and are actually exploring the "planning" phase, then you are in need of immediate assistance. If you get to the point where you feel that you cannot control the urge to harm yourself, you should immediately find a family member to speak with, call a suicide hotline, or call 911. If you are in a situation at home in which you are being abused, another option for help is to call child protective services. Child protective services can arrange for emergency housing to remove you from a dangerous home situation.

It can be scary to pick up the phone and call for help. What happens when you call 911 varies from city to city, but there are usually some similarities. No matter what, some type of emergency response team will come to your house (or to wherever you made the call). This may be the fire department, a paramedic team, the police, or a mental health response team. There is a brief assessment that occurs at your home, but then most often you will be brought to a hospital

Signs That Someone May Be Suicidal

Missing school without being sick

No longer caring about grades

Feeling guilty over trivial things

Losing interest in activities he or she used to enjoy (for example, no longer interested in going out, listening to music, playing computer or video games)

Decreased care paid to hygiene or grooming

Self-harm behavior (for example, cutting legs or forearms)

Using drugs or alcohol without caring about the consequences

setting to meet with a mental health professional for a more intensive interview and assessment. If your community has a mental health response team, then you often do not need to leave your home.

The hospital setting you go to may be a standard medical hospital, or it may be a specialized mental health urgent care setting. These settings often are on the same campus as a hospital, but sometimes they are independent from hospitals. This typically depends on the size of your community. Once at the urgent care, you will often have an intake process completed by a nurse. The mental health professional may be a therapist trained to work in crisis settings or may be a psychiatrist. Regardless of who you see, he or she will meet with you to decide the best treatment plan for the short term. If you have a supportive home environment, often you can meet with the professional and your parents, come up with a plan to get involved in outpatient treatment, and be discharged home from the facility. If your home environment is chaotic with poor support or your urge to harm yourself is too great to control, then you may be admitted to a psychiatric hospital. At a psychiatric hospital, you will usually receive more intensive short-term counseling, meet with a child psychiatrist and social workers, and have parent meetings as well. The goal of a psychiatric hospital stay is to provide short-term treatment and in-depth future planning to eliminate your urge to harm yourself. Treatment to cure depression or anxiety issues takes time—usually three to six months at a minimum. Historically, teens may have stayed in the hospital for this length of time. These days, however, we recognize that such long hospital stays can be extremely disruptive to teens, so the majority of inpatient hospital stays are less than a week, and putting more intensive outpatient treatment plans in place is the goal when teens are hospitalized. In addition, for better or for worse, most insurance companies will no longer pay for long hospital stays.

WHAT YOU NEED TO KNOW

> There are both genetic and environmental risk factors for having significant mental health problems.
> You can learn about your genetic risk factor by educating yourself about people in your family who have had mental health problems.
> Your environmental risk factor for mental health problems is determined by the health of your home and school settings.
> Depression is a common mental illness worldwide and a major source of morbidity for teenagers.
> Common symptoms of depression include suicidal thoughts, being easily irritated, feeling guilty, having poor focus, feeling agitated or jittery, losing interest in activities you used to enjoy, and having problems with sleep or your appetite.
> Anxiety problems are the most common mental health issue in children and teenagers.
> There are many types of anxiety disorders, and all can be affected by bullying. These include generalized anxiety disorder, social phobia, panic disorder, post-traumatic stress syndrome, and obsessive-compulsive disorder.
> There are several different treatments for both anxiety disorders and depression.
> Psychotherapy treatments have good success for treating anxiety and depression. The treatments with the best research in teenagers are cognitive-behavioral therapy (CBT) and interpersonal psychotherapy (IPT).
> Biological treatments for depression and anxiety that have good research to support their use include exercise and medications.
> There are many factors to consider when deciding if medications may be an appropriate treatment for you. Be sure to ask

many questions of your treating doctor to educate yourself well before starting treatment.

➤ There are many different professionals who provide services for teens with mental health issues.

➤ Consistent suicidal or homicidal thoughts or having urges to harm yourself or someone else are a serious warning sign and need immediate attention.

8

Taking Charge Yourself

Suzanne was an outgoing, confident, smart child who excelled in elementary school and middle school. She had several strong friendships, a large group of extended contacts, and good self-esteem. Unfortunately, her father lost his job just after she started ninth grade, and her mother only worked part time. This meant that they could no longer afford to stay where they had been living. Her father was fortunate to find a new job within a month, but it was located in another state. Although Suzanne realized that this move was inevitable and necessary for her family's survival, she was heartbroken at having to leave her friends and familiar surroundings behind. Even harder for Suzanne was the fact that she would have to adjust to starting at new high school in October. How was she going to be able to catch up in time to have friends and do well academically?

Stressed by the moving process, Suzanne began to take solace in food. She would sit among the empty rooms of her old house and open up a giant bag of chips. When she moved into the new place, she would settle into her drab room with a box of delivered pizza. Although she had never been overweight before, she put on 20 pounds in just one month during the moving process. Beyond the visible effect of her weight gain, though, was the invisible damage to her self-esteem.

Starting at her new high school was difficult for Suzanne. She had previously enrolled in the drama club but learned that her new school did not have a drama club or theater group until the spring.

In addition, several of the girls at her new high school decided they didn't like Suzanne and began to mock and tease her during her classes, at recess, and at lunch. Suzanne found herself wandering the campus during recess and lunch, having no one to hang out with. She began to have symptoms of depression, including continued increased appetite, poor sleep, feeling sad most of the time, and even suicidal thoughts. In addition, she had stomachaches and headaches almost daily. Even though her parents sensed something was wrong, Suzanne would lie to them and tell them everything was fine. She didn't want to bother her parents, who were already stressed out with the move and financial problems.

One Monday morning, feeling more stressed than usual, Suzanne decided to skip school. She called the office pretending to be her mother to report herself as being sick. After her parents left for work, she went back to her house and lay down in her bed. She was not aware that her mom was only working until noon that day, and when her mom returned home, she was surprised to find Suzanne in bed. When confronted about not being at school, Suzanne began to cry and finally told her mother about everything she had been dealing with since the family moved. She talked about gaining weight, not being able to make friends, being teased at school, and her symptoms of depression and anxiety. Suzanne's mom was relieved to hear that her daughter was confiding in her, and together they put together a plan.

To begin, both Suzanne and her mother joined a gym. They met with a personal trainer and nutritionist to get some education about diet and exercise, and Suzanne's entire family agreed to work together to be healthier. Next, Suzanne went to speak with her guidance counselor at school. She mentioned the problems with teasing she had experienced and that she had been unable to make new friends. The guidance counselor spoke with her about her interests and felt she may be a good fit for the speech and debate team until the drama club formed in the spring. The counselor also brought in the girls who had been teasing Suzanne, and this put an end to their behavior. Over the next month, Suzanne stuck to her diet and exercise plan and began to enjoy the benefits of getting into shape, including a decrease in her depressive and anxiety symptoms and an increase in her self-esteem. She fit in well in the speech and debate team, and between this club and the gym, she quickly made new friends. She had thought about meeting with a mental health professional, but as her symptoms went away, this was no longer necessary. By the time spring came around, Suzanne had returned to the high-functioning, confident young woman she had been in the past.

On an individual level, the best solution to decrease bullying is to increase your confidence and self-esteem. There are many things you can do to improve these traits. Studies have shown that teenagers who are overweight, obese, or otherwise unhealthy have a higher incidence of being bullied. In the United States, this is an escalating problem, since we now have the highest rate of obesity than at any other time in our history. Some estimates are that as many as one in three teenagers are overweight. These teens are at higher risk for a variety of health problems, including high blood pressure, high cholesterol, diabetes, and even heart disease. If you are feeling unhealthy, it is bad for your self-esteem, which in turn increases the risk for continued poor dietary and exercise habits.

HEALTHY EATING

Teenagers are at high risk for having unhealthy diets. Teens are targeted by advertising from multiple sources. Soft drink and energy drink makers target teenagers as well as fast-food restaurants, which tend to have unhealthy menu items. Although it is beyond the scope of this book to guide you on establishing healthy eating patterns, there are some simple tips that can help you get control over your diet.

The first step is to educate yourself on the basics on how our bodies consume calories. Although there are literally hundreds of diets and theories about the best way to lose weight, there is one basic concept that is easy to learn and can provide a basis for a healthy lifestyle. This concept is "calories in, calories out." No matter what activity you are doing, you are burning calories. Even while sleeping, your body is burning calories. If you did nothing but sleep for 24 hours per day, you would still burn about 1,500 calories. Approximately 3,500 calories is the equivalent of one pound of weight. That means that if you keep your activity level the same, but decrease your food intake by 350 calories each day, then every 10 days you will lose one pound. If you are overweight, then your calorie intake is probably higher than your calorie expenditure. If you need to lose weight, you need to modify your diet or activity level. The two ways to do this are by increasing your activity or decreasing your caloric intake. For teens, since your body is still growing, it is better to increase your exercise or activity level rather than make drastic reductions in your calorie intake. This being said, there may be some dietary changes that are easy to implement and can yield fast benefits.

BEVERAGES

Many teenagers and adults do not realize the amount of calories present in different drinks. A 12-oz. can of soda may have between 130 and 170 calories. In addition, these are "wasted" calories because there is little (if any) nutritional value in sodas, as the calories come from simple sugars. Other high-calorie beverages include juices, coffee drinks, energy drinks, and sports drinks. Sometimes these beverages come in 20-oz. containers. This means that in a single bottle or can there may be 375 to 400 calories. Any caloric beverage that has no nutritional value is a good target for elimination from your diet. Switching your beverage of choice to water can often drastically reduce the amount of calories you are consuming. Do an assessment of what you are drinking, and explore whether this is an area in which you can make some changes.

VEGETABLES

Teens (and adults) tend to snack on unhealthy foods. Potato chips, cookies, candy bars, and high-calorie beverages are common snack items. They have high amounts of nonnutritional calories. The next time you go for a snack, think about trying some vegetables instead. The health benefits of vegetables are many, from decreasing rates of cancer, improving bowel function, and providing vital minerals and vitamins that are especially important during the high-growth phase of your body. In addition, vegetables are a low-calorie food. This means that you could eat about five whole carrots, and this would have the same number of calories as 10 individual potato chips. Even if you do not have a history of trying vegetables or they are connected to bad memories ("Eat your vegetables or no TV!"), it is worthwhile to give them another chance. There are literally hundreds of different vegetables, and with a little trial and error you can find some that you enjoy and that can replace otherwise unhealthy snacks.

LATE-NIGHT EATING

A danger time for unhealthy eating in teenagers is in the late evening or early morning hours, especially if you are working on homework, using your computer, watching television, or playing video games. If you are overweight, one simple restriction that can be helpful is to set a time each night that will be your "cut-off" time for eating. By doing this, you will increase your awareness regarding your nighttime dietary habits. A variation of this theme is to use the "cut-off" time as the time when there will be absolutely no junk food. This would mean replacing high-calorie evening snacks with healthy alternatives.

The Vicious Circle of Bad Health

Thoughts of being unhealthy lead to feelings of depression.

Depression makes you feel tired.

Feeling tired decreases your motivation.

Poor motivation makes it less likely that you will exercise.

Depression can make your body crave unhealthy foods.

Eating unhealthy foods leads to feeling unhealthy.

SKIPPING BREAKFAST

Many teenagers skip breakfast, whether because they are rushed in the morning or they are just not hungry. This is an easy behavior to correct. Most teens are aware of the benefits of eating breakfast. There are clear research studies that demonstrate the importance of having nutrition in the morning. Teens who do not eat anything have a harder time focusing in class, have less energy throughout the day, and do worse on exams. In addition, if you are overweight, skipping breakfast makes it harder to work toward the goal of eating five small meals per day (see below).

EATING TOO QUICKLY

Teen's schedules tend to be packed with many activities. Between school, extracurricular activities, family obligations, work obligations, and friend commitments, there is often little time left in the day. One place that time can be saved is in eating meals. By consuming your meals quickly, you may be able to gain some extra free time. The problem with this is that there is a time delay between eating food and the biochemical feedback between your stomach and brain regarding your hunger "sensor." There is an approximate 20-minute delay between eating food and your brain processing this information to decrease hunger signals. Often it is not just your eating that may occur too quickly, but the eating of your entire family. The next time you eat with your family, time how long everyone is at the table and how long it takes to finish your meal. Practice slowing down

Reading Nutritional Labels	American Heart Association Recommendations
Amount Per Serving	
Tells you the quantity per package that the nutritional information applies to. Sometimes items that you think are only one serving are actually two or more servings, so pay careful attention to this amount.	
Calories/ Calories from Fat	
Tells you the total calories and calories from fat per serving.	Check to see if fat content is less than one third of the total calories. If something is 100 calories, the fat content should be 33 calories or less to meet recommended guidelines.
% Daily Value	
The % daily value is recommended based on a 2000 calorie diet.	
Total Fat	Limit to 25–35% of your total daily calories. There are 9 calories per gram of fat.
Saturated Fat	
This is the main dietary cause of high cholesterol. This type of fat is found mainly in food from animals, including milk products.	Limit to less than 7% of your total daily calories.
Trans Fat	
Trans fat is an "unsaturated" fat that is thought to be more harmful than saturated fats. They tend to raise your bad (LDL) cholesterol and lower your good (HDL) cholesterol.	Recommendation is to keep this below 1% of your total daily caloric intake. This means that if you eat 2,500 calories, you should have no more than 2.5 grams of trans fat.

Reading Nutritional Labels	American Heart Association Recommendations
Polyunsaturated Fat / Monounsaturated Fat	
These are the two unsaturated fats, found in nuts, fish, seeds, and plant oils. Items such as avocados, walnuts, and olive oil contain these fats. These fats may actually help lower your blood cholesterol.	Even though these are known as "good" fats, you still want to limit total fat intake to 25–35% of total calories.
Cholesterol	
A fatty substance that, although being critically important for proper functioning of cells and hormones, can contribute to poor health outcomes. **LDL** cholesterol is "bad" because having high levels of this cholesterol is clearly associated with an increase in cardiovascular disease. **HDL** cholesterol is "good" because it helps prevent atherosclerosis (thickening of artery walls and narrowing of the arteries). It does this by helping the liver remove cholesterol from your blood vessel walls.	Limit to 300 mg a day (unless you have known cholesterol problems).
Sodium	
Sodium regulates blood pressure and blood volume. Sodium occurs naturally in most foods but is also added to many food products to increase flavor. Low-fat foods often contain high amounts of sodium to increase their flavor.	In people without blood pressure, heart, liver, or kidney problems, the recommended sodium intake is 2,300 mg per day.

(continues)

(continued)

Reading Nutritional Labels	American Heart Association Recommendations
Total Carbohydrate	
Carbohydrates are a main dietary component. This category of foods includes sugars, starches, and fiber. The primary function of carbohydrates is to provide energy to the body. There are two main types of carbohydrates—simple and complex. Complex carbohydrates are better for you and are found in fruits, vegetables, whole-grain rice, cereal, and breads. Simple carbohydrates ("Sugars") often are found in candy, sodas, and syrups and lack the vitamins, minerals, and fiber found in complex carbohydrates.	Getting 40–60% of your calories from carbohydrates is recommended. There are 4 calories per gram of carbohydrate.
Dietary Fiber	
Found in fruits, vegetables, and grains, dietary fiber is an important component to a healthy diet. It adds bulk to your diet to help prevent weight gain and treats health conditions, including constipation, diabetes, and heart disease.	The recommendation is 20 to 35 grams per day.
Sugars	
A simple carbohydrate with little nutritional value. These are "empty" calories and can lead to weight gain.	The fewer the better.

Reading Nutritional Labels	American Heart Association Recommendations
Protein	
A complex organic compound contained in every cell in the human body. Protein helps repair cells and make new ones and is especially important in teens to promote proper growth and development.	Your recommended intake of protein depends on your height, weight, and overall health. A general rule is to get about 0.8 to 1.0 grams of protein per kg of weight (see glossary). There are 4 calories per gram of protein.

your chewing, finishing one bite of food before taking another, and using meal times as natural times for conversation with family and friends.

LOSING WEIGHT: BASIC GUIDELINES

These guidelines apply to teens who are trying to lose weight as well as to those who want to adopt a more healthful eating style.

Eat several smaller meals throughout the day. Repeated research into effective eating supports the notion that eating five or six small meals per day leads to improved weight loss, better regulation of metabolism, and improved cognitive functioning (which is important for teens, whose main goal is success at school). The logistics of eating five small meals a day can be challenging. One way to plan your diet is to add two snacks to your day in addition to breakfast, lunch, and dinner. Couple this with decreasing the amount of food you consume at your regular meals, and you will have achieved this goal.

Involve your family. If you are overweight, there is a good chance that one or both of your parents or caregivers is as well. Just as most people understand the dangers of smoking, there are few adults who are unaware of the dangers of being overweight. One of the best interventions for parents to lose weight is to engage them in a program with their children. As a teenager, you can take the lead on changing the eating habits of your family. Sit down with your parents to discuss the idea and do some simple planning. A good start is to open your cabinets and get rid of all the junk food. After this you can plan how to add healthy meals and snacks to your lives.

Watch for "wasted" calories. Wasted calories are those that offer no nutritional benefit. These are usually sugars and fats that are contained in junk food items. Sodas, candy bars, and fried potato chips contain large amounts of these calories. Nutritional labeling has been required on food since 1990. Some states are beginning to adopt other food labeling legislation, including placing nutritional food values on menus at fast-food restaurants. Begin to read these labels and learn how to identify food with little or no nutritional value.

Enjoy "treats" in moderation. There are very few people, let alone teens, who can always eat healthy. This is okay. The key to maintaining your health and enjoying junk food once in a while is moderation. There are different guidelines that you can use to promote moderation with respect to consuming unhealthy food. Two popular methods include picking one day a week in which you can have junk food, or using the 80/20 rule. The 80/20 rule means that 80% of the food that you eat will be in the healthy category, and it is OK if the other 20% falls into the junk food category. Once you have increased your awareness about eating healthy and the nutritional content and calories of different foods, either of these techniques is straightforward to implement.

EXERCISE

Exercise is a powerful intervention. Cardiovascular exercise (such as running, jumping rope, and riding a bicycle) is one of the best activities for your mind and body. Regular exercise can literally cure depression and anxiety for a majority of teenagers. In addition to the health benefits, exercise boosts confidence and self-esteem. Unfortunately, establishing and following through with a regular exercise plan is a difficult task for most people, and this includes teens. Despite this,

Vitamin or Mineral	Significance
Vitamin A (retinol)	Important for the visual cycle. Deficiency can lead to dry eyes, night blindness, skin disorders, infections, diarrhea, and respiratory problems
Calcium	Builds and maintains bones and teeth, regulates heart rhythm, and regulates cell, nerve, and muscle function.
Thiamin (vitamin B1)	Nervous system and muscle functioning and proper functioning of many enzymes. Thiamin deficiency can occur in as little as 15 days and can lead to "beriberi," which causes serious complications in the brain, muscle, heart, and digestive system.
Niacin (nicotinic acid, vitamin B3)	Needed for blood circulation, proper functioning of the nervous system, gastrointestinal tract, and metabolism of proteins and carbohydrates. Niacin is also essential for the synthesis of certain hormones.
Folate	Important for repairing tissues, manufacturing red blood cells, and making DNA.
Zinc	Needed for the functioning of hundreds of enzymes, playing an important role in immune system, taste, smell, and vision processes. Zinc is used as a supplement to treat many illnesses.
Vitamin C (ascorbic acid)	Helps form collagen in bones, cartilage, muscle, and blood vessels. Despite popular perception, research into the health benefits of vitamin C have shown it not effective in preventing or reducing the duration of the common cold.
Iron	Important component of proteins involved in oxygen use in your body. Iron is also needed to synthesize neurotransmitters such as dopamine, norepinephrine, and serotonin.

(continues)

(continued)

Vitamin or Mineral	Significance
Riboflavin	Involved in vital metabolic processes in the body and necessary for cell function, growth, and energy production.
Vitamin B6 (pyridoxine)	Helps maintain functioning of the central and peripheral nervous system, skin, mucous membranes, and blood cell system.
Phosphorous	A mineral critical for energy storage, proper muscle and nerve function, and the formation of bones and teeth (in conjunction with calcium). Having too much or too little phosphorous can cause severe health consequences, including death.

there are steps you can take to increase the likelihood that an exercise plan will be successful.

EDUCATE YOURSELF

If you have access to the Internet or a library, there are literally thousands of resources for learning about exercise. Most exercise plans are individualized—there are few people who have exactly the same workout goals or plan. Just by researching different exercise techniques, you can take notes on which exercise plans are of interest to you. You can then try out the exercises and see which ones are enjoyable and appear to give you the best workout. We recommend having multiple exercise routines as a way to keep your workout interesting and continually work new muscles.

FIND A PARTNER

You are more likely to be consistent in your exercise regimen if you have one or more friends who can join you. Even if they only come occasionally, this extra peer support is a great motivational tool for teens to stay consistent with exercise. Teens who work out with friends tend to push themselves harder and also have someone to provide "spots" as needed when lifting weights.

JOIN A GYM

Although joining a gym does cost money, most parents would be willing to help pay for their children to get in better shape. The YMCA and other community fitness facilities often have programs for teenagers or families that are more affordable than other locations. In addition, gyms tend to offer many fitness classes, some of which may be a good fit for you. Some examples of fitness classes include yoga, kickboxing, step-classes, and circuit training. Not only are these classes a great way to get consistent with exercise, they have the added benefit of introducing you to new people in a nonthreatening environment, which can lead to new friendships.

MORNING VS. NIGHT

The time of day you exercise can make a difference in your success at getting in shape. In general, it is better for your body to work out in the evening, after your muscles are warmed up from a day of activity. The two disadvantages to working out in the evening are that it may cause problems with your sleep if you exercise late at night, and people tend to have a more difficult time being consistent when they exercise in the evenings. Many teens especially have a difficult time being consistent in the evenings because there are usually many other obligations that tend to take priority over working out. These include homework, dinner, friends, and family. Because of this, especially if you do not have family or friend support regarding exercising, you may be better off setting an alarm for a half hour earlier than usual, getting up and immediately starting your exercise routine.

SET REALISTIC GOALS

Many times when teenagers begin workout plans, they may set weight loss goals or strength building goals that are unrealistic to accomplish in the time frame they set for themselves. Our standard recommendation if you need to lose weight is to set a goal of two to three pounds per week. It is unlikely that you would go from not exercising at all to working out six days a week for two hours a session. Instead, start with small goals. Try picking one day during the week to exercise for 30 minutes. If you are successful, add a second day the following week, and then add a third. Research shows that if you can exercise three days a week for 30 minutes, you will gain significant health benefits. This research relates to cardiovascular exercise. Although

Easy Ways to Exercise at Home

Jump rope—You can purchase a good quality jump rope for less than $10. Jumping rope is one of the best exercises for burning calories and your cardiovascular stamina. You can start by setting small goals for yourself. Try jumping rope for one minute at first. If you can successfully do this, begin to increase the amount of time you jump rope each day until you reach 30 minutes.

Yoga—Yoga has been practiced for centuries but recently has gained in popularity. Perhaps no other form of exercise integrates the mind-body connection as well as yoga. Yoga not only increases flexibility, strength, and cardiovascular function but can improve your breathing.

Lifting weights—Even with just a set of five-pound weights and no other equipment, you can put together a workout routine to strengthen all of your major muscle groups. Here are some sample exercises for each muscle group that you can complete with just a set of weights and nothing else:

- ➤ Bicep: standing curls, seated concentrated curls
- ➤ Tricep: tricep kickback, over-the-head extensions
- ➤ Chest: push-ups (no weights needed)
- ➤ Shoulder: straight arm raises, side arm raises, shoulder dumbbell press
- ➤ Back: bent-over row, lying row
- ➤ Leg: squats, lunges

finding 30 minutes may be difficult if you have a busy schedule, you can find time by doing an inventory of your daily routine. Odds are that there is some time you currently spend "relaxing" that you can decrease to make time for exercise. Teenagers in general watch several hours of television each day. See if you can eliminate some of this time to add to exercise. You may be able to combine some television time with exercise. Various ways to exercise while watching television include stationary bikes, elliptical trainers, jump rope, treadmills, and stretching. Although this equipment may be pricey when new, you can usually find used equipment that is in like-new shape from

Checking Your Heart Rate

When beginning an exercise program, you should learn how to check your heart rate. In general, there are two "zones" used to track how well the workout is going. The first zone is commonly referred to as the weight loss zone, and the second is the cardiovascular zone. To check your heart, you first need to find your pulse. Although there are many places you can find your pulse, the most common are on your neck or your wrist. To find your pulse on your wrist, place one or two fingers gently on your wrist just below your thumb. You do not want to push too hard, because that tends to make it more difficult to locate your pulse. If you have a hard time finding your pulse on your wrist, then you can try on your neck. Locate your adam's apple (you can do this by feeling your neck when you are swallowing) and then place one or two fingers to either side of your neck until you feel a pulse. As with your wrist, do not press too hard. In addition to this making it more difficult to find your pulse, if you press too hard you could cause yourself to feel dizzy or possibly faint. Once you have discovered the easiest way to find your pulse, it is simply a matter of finding a clock or watch with a second hand and counting. Count the beats you feel for either 10, 15, or 20 seconds. You then multiply the number of beats you felt by 6, 4, or 3 to get an estimate of the number of beats per minute. The guidelines from the American Heart Association state that your maximum heart rate is about 220 minus your current age. Your heart rate goal during exercise should be between 50% and 85% of your maximum heart rate. For teens, the chart below gives different heart rate guidelines:

	Lower Exercise Range (weight loss zone)	Higher Exercise Range (cardiovascular zone)
Heart Rate	103–144	145–175

sources such as Craigslist, eBay, or your local newspaper. You can take advantage of all the people who bought exercise equipment without proper preparation or dedication and now are looking to recoup some of their losses.

MAKE EXERCISE MORE ENJOYABLE

Play music: If you are fortunate to have an MP3 player such as an iPOD, then you can listen to your favorite sounds while exercising. Music can be especially helpful while exercising because in addition to providing a motivational boost, you are likely to keep pace to the beat of the song you are listening to, which can help you burn more calories.

SELF-DEFENSE

There are many types of self-defense training that you can enroll in. The goal of self-defense training is not to encourage you to engage in physical confrontations with bullies. Rather, it is to provide yourself with the knowledge that you know what to do if you are cornered in a threatening situation. Self-defense builds confidence and focus and can improve academics as well. Self-defense training teaches you how to present yourself in a strong, confident manner. Bullies avoid kids who are confident and carry themselves well. Self-defense training, if done in a group setting, can also lead to new friendships. Self-defense classes provide good cardiovascular and strength training exercise. There are thousands of martial arts studios throughout the United States. In addition, most local community centers and gyms offer martial arts or self-defense training.

A basic tenet of self-defense is to increase your awareness of your surroundings. There are some simple techniques that you can begin to use that can decrease your chance of being victimized. First, always look up when walking. The next time you are at school, the mall, or another busy venue, look around at the people who are walking. You will notice that a large number of the people are watching the ground as they walk. In addition, many people are walking "hunched over" and are not aware of anything going on around them. These people are not only targets for bullies but for other more extreme violence acts (such as a mugging) as well. Convicted criminals have been asked about who they target when looking for victims. Almost unanimously, the criminals report looking for people who watch the ground when they walk or otherwise are not paying attention to their surroundings. Take note of how you carry yourself at school. Do you walk with your eyes on the ground, hoping to avoid seeing kids who may threaten you? Try to keep your head up and stand up straight when you walk. By doing this simple task, you will automatically decrease your appearance as a target. In addition, be aware of what is happening in your immediate environment. If you hear a noise behind you, don't be afraid to turn around to see what is happening. You can check out your environment in a confident manner without instigating trouble.

FRIENDSHIPS

As mentioned earlier, studies have shown that teens who have friends at school are less likely to be victimized than are those without friends. The strength and number of friendships is critical to one's mental health. Although having friends does not necessarily mean that you will never be bullied nor have any mental health problems, if you don't have any friends it almost certainly means that you will. Bullies will usually not target students who are with a group of friends, instead preferring to find kids who are hanging out alone. If you do not have a group of friends at school, then there are steps you can take to remedy this. The key is to find other teens who have similar interests to yours. Practical suggestions for increasing your number of friends or developing new friendships were presented in chapter 4.

APPEARANCE

Part of confidence and self-esteem is learning to take pride in your appearance. This does not mean that you need to own expensive clothes and the latest electronic items. Rather, it means that you should pay attention to basic hygiene. There are two components to your appearance, hygiene and clothing. There are cultural differences in expectations for your hygiene and grooming, and the following are based on the cultural expectations for high school students in the United States.

HYGIENE

The history of hygienic practice in the medical profession is interesting. It was not until the 1900s that someone made the suggestion that doctors should wash their hands after seeing patients. Recognition and implementation of simple hygienic practices led to a drastic reduction in infections. Although it is probably not a matter of life and death if you wash your hands or not, there are health reasons for paying attention to hygiene. Probably the biggest impact from not bathing regularly is an increased risk for skin problems. Once you hit puberty, the hormonal changes in your body increase the formation of sweat glands. This means that even if you are not active during the day, your body is sweating. Not bathing after sweating leads to a high risk for acne and fungal infections (such as athlete's foot). Putting this risk aside, there is a significant social reason for paying attention to hygiene. If you do not bathe and wear deodorant, you will begin to "stink." This may not bother you, but other students and adults will notice this. This will give unnecessary motivation for bullies to tease you. In the broader picture of future goals, not paying attention to hygiene will be a detriment when you ultimately seek employment or to establish new relationships. Showering once a day, combing your hair, and using deodorant to help decrease body odor are important components to presenting yourself in a healthful manner and will minimize the likelihood that you will be targeted by bullies.

CLOTHING

The issue with clothing is straightforward—it is important that your clothes be clean. Inspect your clothes for obvious dirt or stains and then smell them to make sure they are clean. The expectation in high school is that you will wear clean clothes that do not smell. Your parents may take care of this for you. However, if your parents are unwilling or unable to assist you with your laundry and clothing, you can accept this challenge yourself.

ATTITUDE

Your attitude about yourself and your life plays a major role in whether you will be victimized. Understandably, if you have been bullied for an extended period of time and are dealing with other social issues that are making your life stressful, then you may have a negative attitude. You have probably heard the expression "is the glass half full or half empty?" This expression is often used to describe the attitude that people have about life. "The glass half full" people will try to look for the positives in any situation, whereas "the glass half empty" people tend to see only the negative possibilities. Given that there are few positives to situations in which you are being bullied, there are still ways of thinking about situations that may be helpful. To begin, you need to recognize that if you are being bullied, it is the bully who is more likely to suffer negative consequences in the long run for his or her behavior. By reading this book, you will learn the proper steps to take to stop the bullying behavior from continuing. You can change your thought process from that of a victim to someone who knows what to do to solve problems.

WHAT YOU NEED TO KNOW

> If you are being bullied, there are interventions you can do on your own to stop being victimized.

> Adopting healthful eating habits or making a few simple changes to your diet may produce profound results.

> Adding a new exercise plan or increasing your current level of exercise is one of the best things you can do to improve self-esteem.

> Taking self-defense training, either through martial arts or specific self-defense classes, can also increase your self-esteem and decrease the chance that you will be victimized.

> Increasing your friendships will decrease your chances of being bullied.

> Taking pride in your appearance, including grooming and hygiene, will make you less of a target for bullies.

> Having a positive attitude and learning to believe in yourself will improve your confidence and self-esteem.

9

Cyberbullying: The New Frontier

The summer before ninth grade was filled with sun and new experiences for Tiffany. She was hanging out with her group of friends from sixth grade—spending the days at the park with the basketball courts and at the nearby beach. The other kids in her town hung out in the same appealing places as her group. One of the really popular girls from her eighth-grade class, Laryssa, hung out in the "coolest group" and was always nice to Tiffany. When Laryssa would see Tiffany at the beach, she would wave to her and even ask if she wanted to join her group.

Tiffany had always envied the group a little but took solace in knowing that some kids in the group were interested in befriending her. One of the kids who had been talking to her by e-mail and even inviting her to go to the movies was Kevin. Kevin happened to be Laryssa's boyfriend. One day in July, word got out that Laryssa and Kevin had broken up. Vicious rumors began to spread that Tiffany, by befriending Kevin, had "stolen" him and persuaded him to dump Laryssa. Of course, none of this was true, but the rumors continued. Just as the rumors were spreading, Tiffany got a nasty surprise when she logged into her MySpace account. Tiffany's inbox contained four new messages, all from Laryssa. The messages contained threats and mean insults. One of them had hints of real danger, saying that Tiffany better stop talking to Kevin "or else."

With her palms sweating, Tiffany clicked on Laryssa's profile and scrolled down to the comments. Dismayed, she saw that Claire, Laryssa's best friend, had written comments such as "she's such a whore" and "you should beat that slut up." Tiffany clicked on Claire's profile and saw that Tiffany had been continuing the conversation, writing comments such as "she's too fat, she'd probably roll away!" Shuddering, Tiffany signed out of MySpace and ran out of the room. She didn't log in to her MySpace account for days out of fear that there would be more harassing messages. Within those few days, summer vacation ended, and the ninth grade began.

For the first few days of school, Tiffany would enter the campus with the fear of being beat up or cornered by Laryssa and her friends. Two weeks into school, Tiffany's inbox was still flooded with nasty messages. The next weekend, Tiffany went to the movies with two of her friends. She was alarmed to see that Laryssa was there as well. Laryssa marched up to Tiffany, ordered Tiffany's two friends to leave, and stood with her hands on her hips facing Tiffany.

"Hey, Tiffany, isn't that a little too much popcorn you're eating? You should really think about losing some pounds if you even want a chance with Kevin," sneered Laryssa.

Frozen with fear, Tiffany looked around and saw that her two friends were long gone. Laryssa stared her down with the meanest, coldest eyes she had ever seen. All the mean comments were coming to life right in front of her. Laryssa went on about how Tiffany could never get Kevin and that she was stupid for even thinking she had a chance. Laryssa then challenged Tiffany to fight her, saying, "You think you can fight me? Let's go outside!"

Tiffany turned around and ran out of the movie theater. She called her mom and went home. She spent the rest of the weekend moping in her room. She couldn't believe that the horrible words that were circulating on the Internet had come to life.

WHAT IS CYBERBULLYING?

Cyberbullying is a new phenomenon that was first recognized around the turn of the 21st century. With the rise of the Internet, social networking sites, and text messaging, it was only a matter of time before bullying activity would spread to these media. Because cyberbullying takes away the face-to-face aspect of bullying, it has become extremely common. Cyberbullying can be used as both a direct type of bullying and as indirect bullying. Recent cases of cyberbullying (including one in which the mother of a teen created a fake identity to harass one of her daughter's peers, ultimately contributing to her death by suicide) have increased media attention on this topic and raised awareness of this growing trend in bullying. Although the definition of cyberbullying may vary slightly, it ultimately involves the use of electronic means to harass, bully, or otherwise inflict verbal or emotional abuse on another individual.

TEXT MESSAGING

Text messages are sent via cell phones or dedicated texting devices. Text messages are easy to send, and this is a very common technique used in cyberbullying. Common forms of cyberbullying via text messages include sending threatening statements ("You're dead after school") and derogatory comments ("Your clothes suck" or "No one likes u") to an individual. In addition, text messaging can be used to spread false rumors by sending the same text message to multiple people ("Jill reeks today") or to exclude people ("Let's eat lunch at the rally court instead of the quad and not tell Lisa").

SOCIAL NETWORKING SITES

The most popular social networking sites are Facebook and MySpace. Social networking sites, when used for their intended purposes, allow people to share photos, events, and other information with their friends. They are growing in popularity as a way to keep in touch and to meet new people. Unfortunately, as the popularity of these sites grows, so does their ability to be used for cyberbullying. As with Tiffany, cyberbullying can generate large amounts of derisive comments, either directly or indirectly linked to a certain individual. Even if you do not have an account on a social networking site, you may still be subjected to cyberbullying. Other students can use the sites to begin derogatory comments or conversations about you and discuss plans to threaten, harass, exclude, or tease you. In addition, people can post pictures of you that they may have taken without your knowledge. All of these actions fit the definition of cyberbullying.

INSTANT MESSAGING

Instant messaging (IMing) is usually done through software on a computer such as Windows Messenger or America Online (AOL) Instant Messenger. With instant messaging, you log on to your account, and then other people can contact you to share comments while you are both on the computer. Instant messaging can lead to cyberbullying by teens allowing unknown peers access to send messages to them or if someone who was a friend to you in the past suddenly decides to harass you.

CREATING FALSE IDENTITIES

It is not difficult to create a false identity and sign up for a social networking site. At this time, it is not required that social networking

Other Terms for Cyberbullying

Digital bullying

Electronic bullying

E-bullying

Mobile bullying

SMS (short message service) bullying

Computer bullying

Online bullying

Internet bullying

sites confirm the actual identities of their users. Why create a false identity? Unlike text messages or comments made on a social networking site by someone using his or her actual name, if you create a false identity, it can give you a level of anonymity in carrying out cyberbullying. Creating false identities is also common among adults trying to lure teens into dangerous situations.

ASSUMING SOMEONE ELSE'S IDENTITY

For teenagers, assuming another peer's identity while online can be very damaging to the victim. A peer may create a login account on a social networking site using your name or something similar and then proceed to post embarrassing or otherwise hurtful comments under your name. If you are not active on the Internet, you may be unaware that someone has created a "virtual identity" for you and is using it to damage your reputation.

CYBERBULLYING SAFETY TIPS

In addressing cyberbullying, there are some extra tools at your disposal compared with other forms of nonelectronic bullying. Before exploring steps to stop cyberbullying, there are some measures you can take to prevent cyberbullying from occurring. As with most issues that ultimately have an impact on your physical or mental health, using prevention techniques at the beginning can decrease suffering that may occur later.

SAFEGUARD YOUR LOG INS AND PASSWORDS

Although there has been increasing awareness regarding password safety (most sites now require some combination of letters, numbers, and even special symbols in your password), many teens still use passwords that are too easily deciphered. In addition, there are times when you may be using a shared computer (such as at a library) and either forget to sign-out completely from your account or just "close the window" you were working in without signing out. This can result in other people who use the computer next being able to access whatever account you were just in. Always make sure to sign-out and close any windows you are working in. Also make sure that the box that asks you to "Automatically remember your password or log in" is not checked. Even if it is your computer at home, you may not want to check these boxes. If you allow your friends to use your computer or if you are using a computer at another location (including a friend's home), pay careful attention to protecting your log in information.

TAKE ADVANTAGE OF PRIVACY SETTINGS

Every social networking site has privacy settings. When you sign up for one of these sites or for an instant messaging service, review the privacy policy and settings. As a teenager, it is in your best interest to allow only confirmed "friends" to access your information or be able to contact you. Leaving your profile open for all visitors may create extra "views" to your page but will give people access to information about you that is better kept private.

BE CAREFUL WITH WHAT YOU DISCLOSE

Even if you have set careful safeguards on your privacy settings, you still should use common sense when posting information about or pictures of yourself. The general rule of thumb is never to post personal information, such as your telephone number or home address. In addition, use proper judgment when you discuss topics such as sexual activity and substance abuse. Many teens may list information that they think may improve their social status only to find that it is used against them.

LEARN HOW TO "BLOCK" PEOPLE

Every service provider, from cellular phone companies to social networking sites to instant messaging services, allows subscribers to "block" unwanted contact. Before you sign up for a new electronic service, familiarize yourself with what is required to stop unwanted contact. Many times, teens are not aware that it is relatively easy to stop this form of harassment.

BE WARY OF UNKNOWN "FRIENDS"
Even if your privacy settings are set to friends only, you will still receive friend requests from people you don't know. If you receive a friend request from someone you do not definitively know, it is best not to accept.

REPORT EPISODES OF CYBERBULLYING
In addition to blocking unwanted contact, any episodes of cyberbullying (including threats, harassment, teasing, etc) should be reported. There are multiple venues to which you can report cyberbullying. Social networking sites make it simple to report abuse of the system or any inappropriate communications you receive. In addition to reporting to the administrators of the service you are using, you can consider reporting the activity to your school (if the harassment is from a classmate), your parents, and, if the cyberbullying continues or is severe, the police and even the FBI. Most police forces now are set up to handle complaints regarding electronic harassment, and the FBI has a Web site for easy reporting of criminal electronic behavior, including cyberbullying (listed in the resource appendix).

KEEPING TRACK OF BULLYING
Cyberbullying has a major advantage for the victim versus other forms of bullying. This advantage is that it is easier to track and collect data on people who are perpetrating bullying information. This collection of objective bullying information eliminates the issue of students who try to lie or alter events when confronted in other bullying areas. In addition, if the bullying behavior becomes extreme to the point that legal action is needed (either in a criminal manner via the police or a civil manner via lawyers), then having hard copies of actual bullying events makes it much easier for proper corrective action to occur.

TEXT MESSAGES
If you are receiving harassing text messages, DO NOT delete them. There are ways to download the text messages off your phone and preserve copies. It is a good idea to immediately notify your cell phone company that you have been receiving threatening or harassing text messages and that you would like to have them make hard copies of recent text messages.

SOCIAL NETWORKING SITES

All social networking sites have a mechanism to report episodes of harassment or unwanted contact. When you discover that someone has been making inappropriate comments or has posted inappropriate photos, then you should make a hard copy (printout) of the information. You can do this directly from your browser by clicking on the printer icon or going to the File menu and selecting Print. If you are able to, however, it is better to "cut and paste" the offensive information into a word processing document that you can save and then print at a later date. If you do this, make sure to include a notation regarding the date of the information, which sometimes is not obvious based on the material.

INSTANT MESSAGING

As with data from social networking sites, printing information from instant messaging or copying it to a word processing file is the best option for tracking this form of bullying.

LEGAL ISSUES

The Web sites listed in the resource section of this book go into this topic in detail. Because cyberbullying is a relatively new phenomenon, the legal landscape regarding cyberbullying issues is still undergoing changes. Despite this, there are some basic legal issues worth noting. The discussion of items below is not just restricted to cyberbullying but relates to all forms of bullying behavior.

There are two categories of legal charges that can be used when dealing with cyberbullying (as well as other issues). These are *civil* and *criminal.* Criminal law is likely more familiar to you. Criminal law deals with "breaking the law," and there are two classes—misdemeanors and felonies. Robbing a bank, jaywalking, and breaking into your school gym would all result in some type of criminal prosecution. In general, criminal law results in incarceration (serving time in jail or prison) but can also include probation, community services, and paying fines. Some of the common factors in bullying and cyberbullying that can be prosecuted under criminal law include physical violence, threats or coercion (forcing someone to do something against their will by using intimidation), stalking, "hate" crimes, sexual exploitation (including posting sexual images of people), and obscene phone calls. All of these acts should be reported to the police, and the perpetrators can face criminal charges of varying severity for their actions.

Civil law, which is also known as "tort" law, does not result in any type of incarceration or jail time. Successful civil lawsuits result in

What Is a "Hate" Crime?

According to the Federal Bureau of Investigation, a hate crime, also known as a bias crime, is a criminal offense committed against a person, property, or society that is motivated, in whole or in part, by the offender's bias against a race, religion, disability, sexual orientation, or ethnicity/national origin.

the payment of money for a variety of possible damages. In bullying cases, common civil lawsuits that can be filed include defamation of character, intentional infliction of emotional harm, and invasion of privacy (with respect to cyberbullying issues). For teens, civil lawsuits can be brought against the parents of a teenager who is bullying you. This is often a powerful weapon at your disposal in the fight against bullying.

WHAT YOU NEED TO KNOW

- Cyberbullying is a new phenomenon that is growing rapidly with the increased use of electronic forms of communication.
- The most common forms of cyberbullying include text messaging, social networking sites, instant messaging, impersonation, and creating false identities to harass individuals.
- There are many mechanisms to decrease cyberbullying. Tips include safeguarding your accounts and passwords, maintaining high privacy settings, not disclosing personal or embarrassing information, and learning to block unwanted contact.
- Cyberbullying can be tracked easily, and episodes of cyberbullying should be reported to multiple sources, including Internet providers, parents, school staff, and the police, when appropriate.
- There are legal options available in the fight against all types of bullying, including cyberbullying.

10 ▌▌▌

Being an Advocate: Helping Others Cope with Bullying

Marcus had a rough time in elementary school. He was teased for doing well in school, his clothes, his glasses, and having a younger sister who was more popular than he. He got through middle school by sticking with a close group of friends, though he was often physically and verbally harassed by bullies. As he entered high school, a number of things contributed to a drastic improvement in his confidence and self-esteem. He joined the drama club, and his performance in the first school play was outstanding. He also joined the speech and debate team, where he learned to be comfortable speaking in front of people and also won awards at tournaments. He made many new friends from both the drama club and speech and debate team and no longer felt ostracized for doing well in school.

One day, when Marcus was leaving drama rehearsal, he saw that a group of 11th graders had cornered one of his ninth-grade classmates. It was clear that the older students were harassing the ninth grader and preventing him from going home. Seeing this event brought up bad memories from his years of being bullied. In the past, Marcus would have quickly turned the other direction to avoid the possibility that he might be targeted next. This time was different, though. Armed with his new found confidence, Marcus confronted the older students and told them to let the other student leave or he would report their behavior to the principal. Marcus knew that his school had a zero-tolerance program in place to address bullying and that the consequences would be severe for the bullies. When the older students threatened him, Marcus refused to back down and had his cell phone ready to dial 911 if he felt in danger. When the older stu-dents saw that Marcus did not appear intimidated by their threats, they left. Marcus felt good about helping a classmate and had made a new friend for life.

DOING THE RIGHT THING

There are four groups of students when it comes to bullying: bullies, victims, bully-victims, and the "uninvolved" or "bystanders." The majority of students in high school fall into the bystander category. By the time you are in high school, it is almost certain that you have either experienced or witnessed some type of bullying behavior. Most students tend to recall even single episodes of being bullied which would not place them in the scientific classification of being bullied. Even if you have not been repeatedly bullied or bullying has not affected your functioning, if you can remember what you experi-enced, even for a brief moment, while being tormented or watching someone being bullied, then perhaps this can motivate you to stand up for others who are in need of assistance.

WHY TEENS ARE NEEDED TO SOLVE THE PROBLEM

There have been many studies that examine the best way to decrease bullying and create a safe, respectful environment for students to learn throughout elementary, middle, and high school. There are some common themes that have emerged from this research. One of the most important concepts is that to really change a school's attitude, the entire culture around bullying behavior must change. This means that being a bully must no longer have any component of increased social status. Currently, when students are bullies, they often do not meet much resistance from their peers who are unaf-fected by bullying because of their behavior. This may be because other teens are afraid that the bullies may shift their harmful behavior onto them, they may fear for their safety, or they may be afraid they will alienate other students if they confront the bullies. This is most often not the case. If you see something happening at school that you know is wrong, then it is likely that your peers feel the same way. Often it just takes one person to stand up for someone else to rally the support of his or her peers. Although it can be anxiety provoking, if you see another student being victimized and you intervene, you may find that other students pick up on your strength and join you.

Teens are instrumental in changing the culture at schools. Having random assemblies or involving only one group in school communities has not been shown to decrease bullying behavior. What is needed is for all members of the school community to increase their awareness regarding bullying and decide that it will no longer be tolerated. The school community begins with students but extends to teachers, school administrators, and parents. The best chance for changing the culture of your school to one of respect and tolerance is to get all of these groups involved, starting with the teens.

BULLIES NEED HELP, TOO

Teens who are chronic bullies do not do well as adults. Bullies are more likely to use drugs and alcohol, spend time in jail, do poorly in school, and have mental health problems, including depression and anxiety. Although it is a complex set of circumstances that may lead someone to be a bully, most often there is a desire on the part of the bully to change his or her behavior. Many teens who are bullies use their intimidation techniques as a way to keep "forced" friendships. It is unlikely that a teen who is a bully has not experienced some type of suffering in life that has influenced the current behavior. This could include a difficult family or home environment, being abused or bullied by family members, or suffering from mental health issues such as depression or anxiety.

It may take only one person to speak with a bully to change this behavior. Speaking directly to the bully and asking questions in a calm, nonthreatening manner, such as "Why are you a bully?" "Why are you tormenting other people?", or "What can I do to help you so you stop harassing people?" can often lead to dramatic changes in behavior and be the first step toward ending a bully's behavior.

HOW TO TALK TO YOUR FRIEND

If you have a friend who is being bullied or who has been bullied in the past and is now having problems functioning, you should reach out to help. This is true even if it is not one of your "best friends." Being bullied makes teens feel isolated and alone, and any assistance from peers is usually greatly appreciated.

When speaking to a friend about bullying or about concerns for mental health, you need to be aware that it is often embarrassing for teens to acknowledge that they are being victimized. Try to engage your friend in conversation at a low stress time. This will probably be sometime outside of school. In a nonjudgmental manner, initiate a conversation about your concerns regarding your friend. Be direct and honest. Most importantly, be a good listener. Try not to offer immediate advice for the situation. Listen to all the details of the situation, and then offer to help develop a plan of action. You can use information from this book as a guide for what steps need to be taken to resolve the situation.

A WORD ON PERVASIVE DEVELOPMENTAL DISORDERS

There is a psychiatric diagnostic category called pervasive developmental disorders. There are two diagnoses in this category that predispose teens to being bullied. These diagnoses are autism and Asperger syndrome. Sometimes these diagnoses are combined into one term called "autism spectrum disorders." There are two main features of these disorders that are present in teens. The first is impairment of social interactions. This refers to problems in speaking to people, use of nonverbal cues such as eye contact and body language, and not developing proper friendships. The second feature includes preoccupation with certain items, not dealing well with changes in normal routine, or repetitive, odd body movements. These disorders are common, and it is likely that you know someone with some of these behavioral traits. Sometimes teens with autism spectrum disorders are not aware of their diagnosis. If you feel this description of symptoms fits you, there are steps you can take to improve your social interaction skills. Speak with your parents or a school counselor about resources for connecting with someone who specializes in working with teens with autism spectrum disorders.

EMERGENCY SITUATIONS

At some point during your teenage years, you may be speaking with a friend and realize that they are in a dire situation. Remember, suicide is the third leading cause of death for teenagers. Often, as a friend or peer, you may be more clued in than someone's parents as to whether a classmate is in danger of hurting him- or herself. Sometimes a friend may start a conversation with you and say "I want to tell you something but you have to promise not to tell my parents." If this is the case, you should listen to your friend, but if you hear that he or she is thinking of hurting or killing him- or herself, or hurting or killing someone else, you should take this seriously and take action. You will feel much worse about not getting help for a friend who commits suicide than you will about breaking a promise to keep information secret. It may also be possible to let someone know that your friend needs help in an anonymous manner—even a simple phone call to the parents saying that you know their child and are very worried he or she may hurt him- or herself may save a life.

If the situation for harm is imminent and your friend is on the verge of hurting him- or herself, you should call 911 without hesitation. Again, you must balance the risk of your friend being upset (minor damage) at you versus not doing anything and your friend winding up dead (ultimate damage). A call to 911 will usually result in your friend being taken to a hospital for an emergency psychiatric evaluation and can be the first step toward getting treatment that is needed.

WHAT YOU NEED TO KNOW

> The majority of teens are not involved in any type of bullying or victimization.
> In order to "change the culture" of bullying, teens can make the biggest difference.
> Bullies have an increased risk for mental health problems, substance abuse, and winding up in jail than their peers and thus need interventions so they can stop their behavior.
> There are straightforward ways to initiate conversations with peers who may need help.
> Pervasive developmental disorders can make teens more likely to be bullied and require specialized intervention for assistance.
> Take suicidal or homicidal threats seriously, and take steps to save your friends' lives when needed.

Finding and Paying for Care

Hector was a junior in high school in a large metropolitan area. His parents were both immigrants from Mexico, and neither of them had insurance coverage for their children through their jobs. They had applied for Medicaid in the past, but their family income was too high to qualify, thus putting them in the same category as 45 million other people in the United States without health insurance.

Hector had endured harassment through his years in school, both for doing well academically and because he had an uncontrollable motor tic that made him clear his throat over and over again. When his stress level was low, the tic was not noticeable. As Hector became more stressed with college testing coming up, his tic got worse, and this created a cycle of increased bullying, which led to more frequent throat clearing, which further increased the bullying toward Hector. Hector began to experience anxiety and depressive symptoms, resulting in a decrease in his school performance, jeopardizing his plans for his future. Although he knew that his family did not have health insurance, he decided to speak with his school counselor to see if there was any way he could get some help. Although his school did not have services, his counselor was able to give Hector information on a nonprofit agency near his house that worked with teens. In addition, the counselor told Hector that he would intervene to stop the bullying problem. Hector wound up qualifying for reduced-fee services at the clinic near his home, and received individual and group counseling, which got his mental health symptoms under control.

SCHOOL SERVICES

Almost every school has some form of counseling service. Depending on your school, you may have a variety of specialized services available. At a minimum, there will be guidance counselors at your school whom you may have met with regarding your classes. This is a good place to start. You can meet with a guidance counselor and tell him or her that you are having problems that are affecting your schoolwork and were wondering if there were a psychologist you could speak with. Most school districts have psychologists who perform various testing procedures (such as IQ testing), and some schools have masters- or doctoral-level psychologists (or students at these levels) who provide free counseling to any student in need.

MEDICAL INSURANCE

Often, both parents and teens don't realize that medical insurance usually provides coverage for mental health issues. This can include issues that arise for teens when dealing with peer pressure and bullying. If you have medical insurance, examine your insurance card for information on mental health coverage. Although it is not standardized, often the information on mental health and substance abuse coverage is listed on the back of your card. Look for the phrase "MH/SA coverage provided by . . ." Many times, insurance companies "carve-out" their mental health coverage. This means that a different insurance provider than the one that is listed on the front of your card may be listed on the back. The surefire way to check who provides your coverage for mental health counseling is to call the toll-free number and ask.

Historically, mental health and substance abuse coverage has been subject to discriminatory practices by the insurance industry. The good news is that federal legislation was passed in 2008 that has put an end to this policy. Beginning in 2010, there will no longer be imposed limits on mental health or substance abuse treatments. This means there will no longer be limits of 10 or 20 visits per year for mental health issues.

COMMUNITY (NONPROFIT) AGENCIES

If you do not have medical insurance, you can take advantage of services afforded by other agencies. A good starting place is to explore nonprofit counseling agencies in your area. Often you can get a list of these agencies from your school, by doing an Internet search, or

Mental Health Professionals

Title	Degree	Training
Marriage and Family Therapist	M.F.T.	Graduate training program in therapy (classroom study), plus up to two years of clinical training (working with patients)
Social Worker	M.S.W.	Graduate training program (classroom study) in social work, plus up to two years of clinical training (working with patients)
Psychologist	Ph.D., Psy.D.	Extended graduate training program (up to five years) with coursework and clinical training including predoctoral training (usually a one-year internship working with patients before receiving the doctoral degree). After receiving the doctoral degree, there is usually a postdoctoral training period of one year before being licensed to work with patients.
Psychiatrist	M.D., D.O	Completion of medical school (four years) with a four-year residency in general psychiatry. Child psychiatrists may leave the general psychiatry residency after three years and complete a two-year fellowship in child psychiatry for a total of five years of training after medical school.

by checking the phone book for your area. Look for an agency that offers low-cost counseling services. Most of these agencies have sliding-scale services, allowing even people with very little income to afford counseling. There are probably agencies that work exclusively with children and teenagers in your city. In addition to providing individual counseling services, these agencies may have classes or group meetings designed especially to address issues pertinent to teens. Some of these agencies combine mental health treatment with medical care as well, providing routine health exams and treatment when you are ill. Often there is a long wait to receive services at these agencies. Make sure to let them know that you are interested in being on a waiting list, and then check back frequently to see if they have had any cancellations.

COUNTY AGENCIES

Similar to nonprofit agencies, most counties provide services for children, adults, and teens who live in the county. To find out about county services, check the Internet or phone book government section, and look for mental health services under the county heading. To take advantage of these services, you may need to apply for state-assisted health insurance (Medicaid), which varies state to state. County services differ widely, but usually you can obtain some form of individual counseling and medical services, including seeing a psychiatrist.

PASTORAL SERVICES

If you belong to a religious organization (church, mosque, synagogue, etc.), then you may have another set of services available. Many religious organizations have staff who have received special training in counseling and working with teens. Pastoral counseling for mental health issues may be a good starting point, and often you can see someone quickly.

UNIVERSITY TRAINING PROGRAMS

Given the decrease of stigma regarding mental illness and recognition of the health care industry as a stable employment opportunity, there has been an increase in the number of adults training to work in the mental health field. This includes people training to become master's level therapists (social workers or marriage and family counselors), doctoral level psychologists (Ph.D. and Psy.D. degrees), and even more physicians (M.D.s) choosing to specialize in psychiatry since 2000. The benefit to the consumer in the future is that there will continue to be more trained professionals to deliver much-needed mental health care. The immediate benefit for teens who need mental health services is that each of these programs has "trainees" who need time working with clients. In each of the training programs (master's level, doctoral level, or for physicians), students have a number of supervisors who provide guidance while they work with patients. Usually, training programs offer low-cost, sliding-scale, or free services, especially to teens who are willing to work with a trainee. Often, these trainees are very bright and motivated and because they are younger tend to have good connections with teens. Odds are that there are one or more training programs within a reasonable distance of where you live. If you are near any college, university, or professional school, there is a good chance that they will have some type of mental health professional training program. If this is the case, you can call the program to find out about low-cost or free services.

Another venue to receive free mental health care may be through university programs engaged in research programs. Many of the top universities and medical centers are constantly conducting studies into which treatments are effective in decreasing mental health symptoms. If you live near a university with a psychiatry or psychology department, you can call them or search their Web site to see if research subjects are needed.

EMPLOYEE ASSISTANCE PROGRAMS

Depending on the company your parents work for, they may have an employee assistance program (EAP). This means that even though you may not have insurance coverage, you can have up to five free sessions with a mental health professional. Although five sessions may not be enough to provide complete treatment, it is enough to get some guidance on what further steps should be taken to help with current mental health or bullying issues.

WHAT YOU NEED TO KNOW

- ▶ There are many ways to get assistance for issues regarding peer pressure, bullying, or mental health problems.
- ▶ It should be easy to check what services are offered by your school. If it does not provide any, then personnel should have a resource list to point you in the right direction.
- ▶ Medical insurance usually provides coverage for counseling services or for seeing a psychiatrist or other mental health professional.
- ▶ If you do not have medical insurance, you may be able to receive low-cost services from community or county agencies.

You may need to be enrolled in Medicaid to take advantage of county programs.

➤ If you or your family belong to a religious organization, you may be able to get pastoral counseling for free.

➤ University training programs for graduate students or resident physicians often have low-cost or free counseling if you are willing to work with a student.

➤ If your parents work for a company with an employee assistance program, you may be able to get up to five free sessions of counseling.

GLOSSARY

acetylcholine   A neurotransmitter involved in learning, memory, and helping brain cells communicate with each other

atherosclerosis   The process through which fatty plaques cause thickening of the artery walls and narrowing of your arteries. Atherosclerosis increases your risk for heart disease and strokes.

blood pressure   A measure of the pressure of your blood as it travels through your blood vessels. The top number is your systolic blood pressure and indicates the pressure of blood in your vessels when your heart beats. The bottom number is your diastolic blood pressure and indicates the pressure of blood in your vessels when your heart relaxes. Blood pressure increases when you are overweight or do not exercise. Although guidelines vary based on your age, normal blood pressure is considered less than 120 (systolic)/ 80 (diastolic). If your blood pressure is higher than 140/90, then you have high blood pressure and should see your doctor.

bullying   Behavior designed to harm another individual through verbal, emotional, or physical means. The behavior must be repeated over time, and there must be a difference in power (or social status) between the perpetrator (bully) and the victim.

"carve-out"   A term used to describe how insurance companies sometimes contract with other agencies to provide some of their services (often mental health or substance abuse)

catecholamines   A group of neurotransmitters and hormones produced in the adrenal gland that have important physiological effects. Norepinephrine and dopamine are examples of catecholamines.

civil law   Also known as "tort" law, people who are bullied may be eligible to sue for damages for actions such as defamation of character, intentional infliction of emotional harm, or privacy invasion (in the case of cyberbullying). Civil law never results in people being incarcerated (going to jail).

criminal law   When bullying behavior involves actions such as threats, obscene phone calls, stalking behavior, physical violence, and other similar events, then criminal charges can be filed against the perpetrators. Criminal law usually results in probation, jail time, or possibly fines or community service.

cyberbullying   Using electronic means to harass, bully, or otherwise inflict verbal or emotional abuse on another individual

direct bullying   Bullying that consists of direct threats of violence or actual physical harm

dopamine   A neurotransmitter responsible for mediating several functions in the brain. This neurotransmitter is the source of the "high" feeling and addictive properties of many illicit drugs.

endorphins   A neurochemical that occurs naturally in the brain that can produce a decrease in pain and a pleasurable effect

indirect bullying   Bullying that consists of spreading rumors, excluding people from activities, or teasing

inpatient   A term that refers to psychiatric treatment that takes place in a hospital or residential setting

kilogram   A metric unit of weight. To convert your weight from pounds to kilograms, divide your weight in pounds by 2.2.

morality   The distinction between the concepts of good and evil or right and wrong. Although there may be general beliefs regarding morality, it is a trait that varies from person to person.

morbidity   A measure of suffering, including such things as days lost from school or work and physical or mental pain

neurotransmitter   A chemical substance that transmits nerve signals across a synapse

norepinephrine   A neurotransmitter involved in many functions in the human mind and body. In addition to affecting heart rate and blood pressure, norepinephrine has been implicated in depression and in difficulties with attention.

outpatient   A term that refers to mental health treatment that happens at a clinic location, with the patient spending the rest of the time in usual locations (home and school). In intensive outpatient treatment, you may spend anywhere from three to eight hours per weekday in a treatment setting but sleep at home.

pharmacotherapy   A treatment plan consisting of education about and the use of medications to treat mental health symptoms

psychoeducation   Education regarding various psychiatric illnesses, symptoms, diagnoses, and the treatment options for each. This includes estimated success rates for therapy and medication treatments and side effects of medications.

peer pressure   When a decision or action you make is influenced significantly by your perception of what other people will think about you. Peer pressure can be positive (studying hard for a test because you want your peers to think highly of you) or negative (trying drugs or alcohol to fit in).

rapport   A measure of trust and comfort with another individual. This is used to assess how well your therapy treatment may work.

schizophrenia   A severe illness in which people experience psychotic symptoms. Typical symptoms include hearing voices, being unable to think clearly, and feeling paranoid.

synapse   The gap between the terminal end of one nerve cell and the receptor end of another nerve cell

serotonin   A neurotransmitter that regulates many functions. Serotonin is known to affect mood, anxiety levels, sleep, and sensory perception.

APPENDIX

Helpful Organizations

CYBERBULLYING
The Internet Crime Complaint Center
http://www.ic3.gov
*The Internet Crime Complaint Center (IC3) is a partnership between
the Federal Bureau of Investigation (FBI), the National White
Collar Crime Center (NW3C), and the Bureau of Justice Assistance
(BJA). IC3's mission is to serve as a vehicle to receive, develop,
and refer criminal complaints regarding the rapidly expanding
arena of cybercrime. The IC3 gives the victims of cybercrime
a convenient and easy-to-use reporting mechanism that alerts
authorities of suspected criminal or civil violations. For law
enforcement and regulatory agencies at the federal, state, local,
and international levels, the IC3 provides a central referral
mechanism for complaints involving Internet-related crimes*

Wired Safety
http://www.wiredssafety.org
*WiredSafety is a 501(c)(3) program and the largest online safety,
education, and help group in the world. It is a cyberneighborhood
watch and operates worldwide in cyberspace through more than
9,000 volunteers. (WiredSafety is run entirely by volunteers.) Its
work falls into four major areas:*

- *help for online victims of cybercrime and harassment*
- *assisting law enforcement worldwide on preventing and
  investigating cybercrimes*
- *education*
- *providing information on all aspects of online safety,
  privacy, and security*

There is a Cyber911 help line that gives netizens access to help when
they need it online. This includes information on cyberbullying and

how to report it and other valuable resources for protecting yourself when using the Internet.

Connect Safely

http://www.connectsafely.org

ConnectSafely is for parents, teens, educators, advocates— everyone engaged in and interested in the impact of the social Web. The user-driven, all-media, multiplatform phase of the Web has begun, we all have much to learn about it, and this is the central space—linked to from social networks across the Web—for learning about safety on Web 2.0 together. The forum is also designed to give teens and parents a voice in the public discussion about youth online safety begun back in the '90s. In addition, the site has tips for teens and parents as well as other resources for safe blogging and social networking. ConnectSafely.org is a project of Tech Parenting Group, a nonprofit organization based in Palo Alto, Calif., and Salt Lake City, Utah.

BULLYING

U.S. Department of Health and Human Services: Stop Bullying Now

comments@hrsa.gov

http://Stopbullyingnow.hrsa.gov

This Web site has valuable information about bullying, children who are bullied, and children who bully. You will also find tips and suggestions on how you can use this site to prevent bullying in your community.

National Crime Prevention Council

2345 Crystal Drive

Suite 500

Arlington, VA 22202

(202) 466-6272

http://www.ncpc.org

The National Crime Prevention Council's mission is to be the nation's leader in helping people keep themselves, their families, and their communities safe from crime. To achieve this, NCPC produces tools that communities can use to learn crime prevention strategies, engage community members, and coordinate with local agencies.

Bully Police USA
http://www.Bullypolice.org
Bully Police is a watchdog organization that advocates for bullied children and reports on state antibullying laws. This site gives each state grades for its laws regarding bullying. It has links to the actual laws in each state on bullying. It also has links to resources for parents and teens as well as to bullying support groups.

International Bullying Prevention Association
P.O. Box 2288
Falmouth, MA 02536
(508) 274-8246
http://www.stopbullyingworld.org
The mission of the International Bullying Prevention Association is to support and enhance quality, research-based bullying prevention principles and practices in order to achieve a safe school climate, healthy work environment, good citizenship, and civic responsibility.

The Partnership for Families and Children
450 Lincoln Street, Suite 100
Denver, CO 80203
(303) 837-8466
info@pffac.org
http://www.pffac.org
The Partnership for Families and Children is an independent nonprofit provider of capacity-enhancing services, research, and evaluation in the area of child and family health and well-being, serving as a trusted partner for social change and bullying prevention.

Stop Bullying Now!
409 North Wayne Road
Wayne, ME 04284
stan@stopbullyingnow.com
http://www.stopbullyingnow.com
The Stop Bullying Now Web site aims to help stop bullying in schools and communities. At this Web site, information on what works to stop bullying, and what doesn't, and training materials are available. Information is provided for teachers, administrators, parents, and youths.

Center for Safe Schools
275 Grandview Avenue Suite 200
Camp Hill, PA 17011

(717) 763-1661
www.safeschools.info
*The Center for Safe Schools seeks creative and effective solutions to
problems that disrupt the educational process and affect school
safety. Training, technical assistance, and a clearinghouse of
video and print materials are available through the center to help
schools identify and implement effective programs and practices.
The center also maintains a database of resources available to
assist school districts.*

Jeremiah Project 51
Winnetka, CA 91330-0001
(866) 721-7385
info@jeremiah51.com
http://www.jeremiah51.com
*Jeremiah Project 51 is determined to attack and defeat bullying one
school district at a time until bullying has been eliminated from
all schools. Founded by an individual with personal experience of
the devastation that bullying can cause, Jeremiah Project 51 is a
nonprofit organization dedicated to bullying prevention. This Web
site provides resources for students and parents, including toll-free
numbers for support.*

PEER PRESSURE / TEEN ISSUES
Medline Plus Teen Health
8600 Rockville Pike
Bethesda, MD 20894
http://www.nlm.nih.gov/medlineplus/teenhealth.html
*A service of the U.S. National Library of Medicine and the National
Institutes of Health, this Web site provides scientific information
on multiple issues regarding teenagers and teen development.
Topics discussed include mental health, sexual health, preventive
health, and many others. Glossaries and dictionaries are just some
of the reference materials found on this Web site.*

Go Ask Alice!
http://goaskalice.columbia.edu
*Columbia University's health question-and-answer service for teens.
This site contains information and resources on alcohol and other
drugs, fitness, nutrition, emotional health, general health, and
sexuality and relationships. Teens can submit their questions on
any topic to get advice.*

Teen Growth

11274 West Hillsborough Avenue
Tampa, FL 33635
feedback@teengrowth.com
http://www.teengrowth.com

*TeenGrowth is a unique and interactive Web site specifically tailored
toward the health interests and general well-being of the teenage
population. TeenGrowth offers a secure environment to search
for, request, and receive valuable health care information on
topics such as alcohol, drugs, emotions, health, family, friends,
school, sex, and sports. TeenGrowth is one of the few Internet
sites that focuses exclusively on the educational health issues
of adolescents. The medical advisory board, consisting of well-
known and respected physicians in the pediatric community,
oversees all content on the site, thereby guaranteeing its medical
accuracy.*

Teens Health

Nemours Foundation
http://kidshealth.org/teen/

*TeensHealth was created for teens looking for honest, accurate
information and advice about health, relationships, and growing
up. It is a safe, private place that's accessible 24 hours a day to
get the doctor-approved info you need to understand the changes
that you (or your friends) may be going through—and to make
educated decisions about your life. There's a lot of confusing,
misleading, and just plain wrong health information on the Web,
and the site's mission is to tell it to you straight.*

Girls Health

8270 Willow Oaks Corporate Drive
Suite 301
Fairfax, VA 22031
http://4girls.gov

*The mission of Girlshealth.gov, developed by the Office on Women's
Health in the Department of Health and Human Services, is to
promote healthy, positive behaviors in girls between the ages of
10 and 16. The site gives girls reliable, useful information on the
health issues they will face as they become young women and tips
on handling relationships with family and friends at school and
at home. Information and resources on fitness, nutrition, illness,
drugs, alcohol, smoking, bullying, and safety are provided on this
Web site.*

National Mental Health Information Center
P.O. Box 2345
Rockville, MD 20847
(800) 789-2647
http://mentalhealth.samhsa.gov
The National Mental Health Information Center's missions are to
teach young people how to refuse offers for cigarettes, alcohol,
and drugs; talk to young people about how to avoid undesirable
situations or people who break the rules; remind children that
there is strength in numbers; and let young people know that it is
OK to seek adult advice and to nurture strong self-esteem.

SUBSTANCE USE

National Institute on Drug Abuse (NIDA) for Teens
National Institutes of Health (NIH)
9000 Rockville Pike
Bethesda, MD 20892
http://Teens.drugabuse.gov
The National Institute on Drug Abuse (NIDA), a component of
the National Institutes of Health (NIH), created this Web site to
educate adolescents ages 11 through 15 (as well as their parents
and teachers) on the science behind drug abuse. NIDA enlisted
the help of teens in developing the site to ensure that the content
addresses appropriate questions and timely concerns. Recognizing
that teens want to be treated as equals, NIDA scientists were
careful not to preach about the dangers of drug use. Rather, the
site delivers science-based facts about how drugs affect the brain
and body so that kids will be armed with better information to
make healthy decisions. Elements such as animated illustrations,
quizzes, and games are used throughout the site to clarify
concepts, test the visitors' knowledge, and make learning fun
through interaction.

Teens Against Drunk Driving
T.A.D.D. Teens Against Drunk Driving
8827 West Ogden Avenue, Suite 177
Brookfield, IL 60513
(888) 318-TADD
info@teensagainstdrunkdriving.org
http://www.teensagainstdrunkdriving.org
Teens Against Drunk Driving, Inc. (T.A.D.D.) is a not-for-Profit
community service organization that provides high schools with

a safe driving program that is incorporated into a homework planner and study guide for high school students.

Freevibe
National Youth Anti-Drug Media Campaign
Drug Policy Information Clearinghouse
P.O. Box 6000
Rockville, MD 20849-6000
Phone: (800) 666-3332
http://www.freevibe.com
Freevibe.com was created for the National Youth Anti-Drug Media Campaign, a program of the Office of National Drug Control Policy. Freevibe's goal is to provide teens with the knowledge and personal empowerment to reject drug use and other risky behaviors. Freevibe.com is updated regularly with the latest national statistics on teen drug abuse and other relevant trends and also incorporates insights and feedback from site visitors. Freevibe contains information and resources to help you or your friends become knowledgeable about substance use and have tools to quit.

National Council on Alcoholism and Drug Dependence, Inc.
244 East 58th Street, 4th Floor
New York, NY 10022
(212) 269-7797 or (800) NCA-CALL (24-hour affiliate referral)
national@ncadd.org
http://www.ncadd.org
Founded in 1944 by Mrs. Marty Mann, a pioneer in the alcoholism field, the National Council on Alcoholism and Drug Dependence, Inc. (NCADD) provides education, information, help, and hope to the public. It advocates prevention, intervention, and treatment through a nationwide network of affiliates. In addition, NCADD operates a toll-free Hope Line (800-NCA-CALL) for information and referral and a National Intervention Network (800-654-HOPE) to educate and assist the families and friends of addicted persons.

Partnership for a Drug-Free America
405 Lexington Avenue, Suite 1601
New York, NY 10174
(212) 922.1560
http://checkyourself.com
http://www.drugfree.org
The Partnership for a Drug-Free America is a private nonprofit organization that unites communications professionals, renowned

scientists, and parents in the mission to reduce illicit drug abuse in America. Drugfree.org is a drug abuse prevention and treatment resource, existing to help parents and caregivers effectively address alcohol and drug abuse with their children. This Web site gives families the tools, information, and support they need to help their children lead healthy, drug-free lives.

Drug Strategies
1616 P Street NW, Suite 220
Washington, DC 20036
(202) 289-9070
dspolicy@aol.com
http://www.bubblemonkey.com
http://www.drugstrategies.com
A nonprofit research institute that promotes more effective approaches to the nation's drug problems and supports private and public efforts to reduce the demand for drugs through prevention, education, treatment, law enforcement, and community initiatives. Bubble monkey is an interactive site for teens with information and resources on many different drugs of abuse.

MENTAL HEALTH AND SUICIDE
American Foundation for Suicide Prevention
120 Wall Street, 22nd Floor
New York, NY 10005
(212) 363-3500 or (888) 333-AFSP (2377)
inquiry@afsp.org
http://www.afsp.org
The American Foundation for Suicide Prevention (AFSP) is the leading national not-for-profit organization exclusively dedicated to understanding and preventing suicide through research and education and to reaching out to people with mood disorders and those impacted by suicide.

SAVE: Suicide Awareness Voices of Education
8120 Penn Avenue South, Suite 470
Bloomington, MN 55431
Phone: (952) 946-7998
http://www.save.org
SAVE was one of the nation's first organizations dedicated to the prevention of suicide and was a cofounding member of the National Council for Suicide Prevention. Its history and growth

from an all-volunteer, small grassroots group of passionate survivors led it to become what is one of today's leading national not-for-profit organizations with staff dedicated to prevent suicide. This site, along with its work, is based on the foundation and belief that suicide should no longer be considered a hidden or taboo topic and that through raising awareness and educating the public, we can SAVE lives.

Suicide Prevention Action Network USA
1025 Vermont Avenue NW, Suite 1066
Washington, DC 20005
(202) 449-3600
info@spanusa.org
http://www.spanusa.org
The Suicide Prevention Action Network USA (SPAN USA) is a 501(c)(3) organization dedicated to preventing suicide through public education and awareness, community action, and federal, state, and local grassroots advocacy.

Suicide Prevention Resource Center
Education Development Center, Inc.
1000 Potomac Street NW, Suite 350
Washington, DC 20007
(877) GET-SPRC [438-7772]
http://www.sprc.org
SPRC promotes the implementation of the National Strategy for Suicide Prevention and enhances the nation's mental health infrastructure by providing states, government agencies, private organizations, colleges and universities, and suicide survivor and mental health consumer groups with access to the science and experience that can support their efforts to develop programs, implement interventions, and promote policies to prevent suicide.

Suicide Prevention Services
Stone Manor
528 South Batavia Avenue
Batavia, IL 60510
(630) 482-9696
http://www.spsfv.org
Suicide Prevention Services is dedicated to the mission of reducing and eliminating suicide and suicide attempts through education, advocacy, and collaboration.

Canadian Association for Suicide Prevention
870 Portage Avenue
Winnipeg, MB, R3G 0P1
(204) 784-4073
http://www.casp-acps.ca
The Canadian Association for Suicide Prevention (CASP) was incorporated in 1985 by a group of professionals who saw the need to provide information and resources to communities to reduce the suicide rate and minimize the harmful consequences of suicidal behavior. We, like many others, envision a world in which people enjoy an optimal quality of life, are long-living, socially responsible, and optimistic about the future.

Youth Suicide Prevention Program
444 Northeast Ravenna Boulevard, Suite 401
Seattle, WA 98115
(206) 297-5922
info@yspp.org
http://www.yspp.org/
YSPP envisions a state where youth suicide is a rare event, where young people are nurtured and supported, where individuals and families are aware of risk factors for suicide and actively seek help from accessible, effective community resources.

Kids Crisis
2969 Main Street
Buffalo, NY 14214
(877) KIDS-400
info@kidscrisis.com
http://www.kidscrisis.com
The Kids Helpline is a program within the Suicide Prevention and Crisis Services, Inc., agency. It is a unique, private nonprofit mental health and human service agency dedicated to promoting the health, safety, and well-being of the community through prevention, education, immediate intervention, and access to communitywide resources 24 hours a day. In addition to crisis services, some of the other topics covered on this Web site for teens include bullying, drug use, eating disorders, and other mental health issues.

SEXUALITY, PREGNANCY, AND SEXUALLY TRANSMITTED DISEASES
Teenwire.com
Planned Parenthood Federation of America

434 West 33rd Street
New York, NY 10001
http://www.teenwire.com

*Teenwire.com is an award-winning sexual health Web site for teens.
They are committed to giving you the facts about sex so that you
can use this information to make your own responsible choices.
They provide honest and nonjudgmental information about
sexuality in language you can understand with the hope that
you will use this knowledge to reduce your risk of unintended
pregnancy and sexually transmitted infections.*

Advocates for Youth
2000 M Street NW, Suite 750
Washington, DC 20036
(202) 419-3420
http://www.advocatesforyouth.org/youth/index.htm

*Advocates for Youth is dedicated to creating programs and
advocating for policies that help young people make informed
and responsible decisions about their reproductive and sexual
health. Advocates provide information, training, and strategic
assistance to youth-serving organizations, policy makers, youth
activists, and the media in the United States and the developing
world.*

American Social Health Association
P.O. Box 13827
Research Triangle Park, NC 27709
(919) 361-8488
(800) 227-8922 [STI Resource Center Hotline]
teen-stinet@ashastd.org
http://www.iwannaknow.org/
http://www.ashastd.org/

*Since 1914, the American Social Health Association (ASHA)
has been dedicated to improving the health of individuals,
families, and communities, with a focus on preventing sexually
transmitted diseases and infections (STDs/STIs) and their harmful
consequences. These sites have the facts, the support, and the
resources to answer your questions, find referrals, join support
groups, and get access to in-depth information about sexually
transmitted infections. The information you find on these Web
sites is based upon well-researched and documented medical facts
and follows approved treatment guidelines as recommended by the
Centers for Disease Control and Prevention.*

Cool Nurse
Hillclimb Media
710 Second Avenue
Suite 1130
Seattle, WA 98104
http://www.coolnurse.com
Cool Nurse was created to help today's teens and young adults
achieve and maintain a high level of health, fitness, and well-
being. Teenagers need to know the latest about health and about
their bodies. Health and sex education has been cut from many
school budgets. This site is a guide to assist you in making
intelligent, informed decisions. Everyone at Cool Nurse volunteers
time, and the site has been a collaborative effort.

Sex, etc.
Rutgers University
41 Gordon Road, Suite C
Piscataway, NJ 08854
sexetc@rci.rutgers.edu
http://www.sexetc.org
Sex, Etc. is an award-winning national magazine and Web site on
sexual health that is written by teens, for teens. It is part of the
Teen-to-Teen Sexuality Education Project developed by Answer
(formerly the Network for Family Life Education), a leading
national organization dedicated to providing and promoting
comprehensive sexuality education. Answer is part of the Center
for Applied Psychology at Rutgers, The State University of New
Jersey.

DIET AND EXERCISE
Nutrition.gov
National Agricultural Library
Food and Nutrition Information Center
Nutrition.gov Staff
10301 Baltimore Avenue
Beltsville, MD 20705-2351
http://www.nutrition.gov
Nutrition.gov provides easy access to the best food and nutrition
information from across the federal government. It serves as a
gateway to reliable information on nutrition, healthy eating,
physical activity, and food safety for consumers. Providing
science-based dietary guidance is critical to enhance the public's

ability to make healthy choices in the effort to reduce obesity and other food related diseases. Since dietary needs change throughout the lifespan, specialized nutrition information is provided about infants, children, teens, adult women and men, and seniors. Users can find practical information on healthy eating, dietary supplements, fitness, and how to keep food safe. The site is kept fresh with the latest news and features links to interesting sites.

The President's Council on Physical Fitness and Sports
Department W
200 Independence Avenue SW
Room 738-H
Washington, DC 20201-0004
(202) 690-9000
http://www.presidentschallenge.org/home_teens.aspx
http://www.fitness.gov
The health, physical activity, fitness, and sports information Web site of the President's Council on Physical Fitness and Sports. You can find out about the council and its work, view publications, and link to the resources of other government agencies as well as to health and fitness organizations. To find out how you can start a physical activity program today and stay active and fit for life while earning presidential awards, visit the free, interactive physical activity and fitness Web site, http://www. presidentschallenge.org.

MyPyramid.gov
USDA Center for Nutrition Policy and Promotion
3101 Park Center Drive
Room 1034
Alexandria, VA 22302-1594
(888) 7-PYRAMID
Support@cnpp.usda.gov
http://www.mypyramid.gov
The Center for Nutrition Policy and Promotion, an organization of the U.S. Department of Agriculture, was established in 1994 to improve the nutrition and well-being of Americans. Toward this goal, the center has developed MyPyramid.Gov to provide guidance for adults, teenagers, and children on developing healthy nutritional habits.

Spark Teens
SparkPeople Inc.
4392 Marburg Avenue
Cincinnati, OH 45209
http://www.sparkteens.com

At SparkPeople, the mission is to SPARK millions of PEOPLE to reach their goals and lead healthier lives. They offer nutrition, health, and fitness tools, support, and resources that are 100% free. Their weight loss program teaches people to stop dieting and transition to a permanent, healthy lifestyle. Far beyond just weight loss, SparkPeople helps everyone learn to eat better and exercise regularly—for life. And people who don't want to lose weight can still join and benefit from SparkPeople's tools, resources, and community features. In addition to informative articles and interactive tools, such as fitness trackers and meal plans, members can find support and encouragement from the vibrant, positive community of members and experts. All the components of the program mix in an element of fun so that members truly do stick with their programs. With millions of members, there have been thousands of success stories firsthand. SparkTeens is dedicated to helping teens reach their diet and nutrition goals.

READ MORE ABOUT IT

BULLYING

Aidoff, Jaime. *Names Will Never Hurt Me*. New York: Puffin, 2005.

Butler, Dori Hillstad. *The Truth about Truman School*. Morton Grove, Ill.: Albert Whitman & Company, 2009.

Carter, Jay. *Nasty People*. New York: McGraw-Hill, 2003.

Coloroso, Barbara. *The Bully, the Bullied, and the Bystander*. New York: HarperCollins, 2004.

Covey, Stephen. *The Seven Habits of Highly Effective Teens*. New York: Fireside, 1998.

Grasso, Joe. *Don't Bully My Kids* (DVD with Self-Defense and Exercise Training). San Jose, Calif.: Dontbullymykids.com, 2007.

Donahue, John. *Till Tomorrow*. New York: Farrar, Straus & Giroux, 2001.

Dubin, Nick. *Asperger Syndrome and Bullying: Strategies and Solutions*. London: Jessica Kingsley, 2007.

Elliot, Pursell. *School Mobbing and Emotional Abuse: See It—Stop It—Prevent It with Dignity and Respect*. New York: Brunner-Routledge, 2003.

Ferrara, Judith. *Peer Mediation*. Portland, Maine: Stenhouse, 1996.

Field, Evelyn. *Bully Blocking: Six Secrets to Help Children Deal with Teasing and Bullying*. London: Jessica Kingsley Publishers, 2007.

Flake, Sharon. *The Skin I'm In*. New York: Jump at the Sun/Hyperion, 1998.

Fox, Annie. *Can You Relate?: Real-World Advice for Teens on Guys, Girls, Growing Up, and Getting Along*. Minneapolis: Free Spirit Publishing, 2005.

Fox, Annie. *The Teen Survival Guide to Dating & Relating: Real-World Advice on Guys, Girls, Growing Up, and Getting Along*. Minneapolis: Free Spirit Publishing, 2005.

Hinduja, Sameer, and Justin Patchin. *Bullying Beyond the Schoolyard: Preventing and Responding to Cyberbullying*. Thousand Oaks, Calif.: Corwin Press, 2008.

Kaufman, Gershen, Lev Raphael, and Pamela Espeland. *Stick Up For Yourself*. Minneapolis: Free Spirit Publishing, 1999.

Kowalski, Robin, Susan Limber, and Patricia Agatsob. *Cyber Bullying: Bullying in the Digital Age.* Hoboken, N.J.: Wiley-Blackwell, 2008.

Michael de Guzman. *Melonhead.* New York: Farrar, Straus & Giroux, 2002.

Miller, Deanna. *Time to Tell 'Em Off! A Pocket Guide to Overcoming Peer Ridicule.* Deanna Miller, 2002.

Mills, Claudia. *Lizzie at Last.* New York: Farrar, Straus & Giroux, 2000.

Nixon, Charisse, and Cheryl Dellasega. *Girl Wars: 12 Strategies That Will End Female Bullying.* New York: Fireside, 2003.

Noll, Kathy, and Jay Carter. *Taking the Bully by the Horns (Children's Version of Dr. Jay Carter's Best-selling Book, Nasty People).* London: Unicorn Press, 2003.

Peretti, Frank. *No More Bullies: For Those Who Wound or Are Wounded.* Nashville: Thomas Nelson Publisher, 2003.

Pownall-Gray, Dickon. *Surviving Bullies Workbook: Skills to Help Protect You from Bullying.* lulu.com, 2006.

Romain, Trevor. *Cliques, Phonies, and Other Baloney.* Minneapolis: Free Spirit, 1998.

Simmons, Rachel. *Odd Girl Out.* Orlando, Fla.: Harcourt, 2003.

———. *Odd Girl Speaks Out.* Orlando, Fla.: Harcourt, 2004.

Wilhelm, Doug. *The Revealers.* New York: Farrar, Straus & Giroux, 2003.

Willard, Nancy. *Cyber-Safe Kids, Cyber-Savvy Teens: Helping Young People Learn to Use the Internet Safely and Responsibly.* San Francisco: Jossey-Bass, 2007.

Winkler, Kathleen. *Bullying: How to Deal With Taunting, Teasing, and Tormenting.* Berkeley Heights, N.J.: Enslow Publishing, 2005.

Wiseman, Rosalind. *Queen Bees and Wannabes.* London: Piatkus Books, 2003.

Youth Communication. *Sticks and Stones: Teens Write About Bullying.* New York: Youth Communication, 2005.

HAZING

Apostolina, M. *Hazing Meri Sugarman.* New York: Simon Pulse, 2005.

Guynn, Kevin L., and Frank D. Aquila (illustrator). *Hazing in High Schools: Causes and Consequences.* Bloomington, Ind.: Phi Delta Kappa Educational Foundation, 2005.

Hamilton, Jill. *Bullying and Hazing (Issues That Concern You).* Farmington Hills, Mich.: Greenhaven Press, 2008.

Nuwer, Hank. *Broken Pledges: The Deadly Rite of Hazing.* Atlanta: Longstreet Press, 1990.

————. *High School Hazing: When Rites Become Wrongs.* London: Franklin Watts, 2000.

————. *Wrongs of Passage: Fraternities, Sororities, Hazing and Binge Drinking.* Bloomington: Indiana University Press, 2002.

Scleifer, Jay. *Everything You Need to Know About the Dangers of Hazing.* New York: Rosen Publishing Group, 1996.

PEER PRESSURE

Anderson, Carol B. *Let's Talk About Peer Pressure.* Montgomery, Ala.: E Booktime LLC, 2007.

Carlson, Richard. *Don't Sweat the Small Stuff for Teens Journal.* New York: Hyperion, 2002.

Cherniss, Hilary, and Sara J. Sluke. *The Complete Idiot's Guide to Surviving Peer Pressure for Teens.* Royersford, Pa.: Alpha, 2001.

Carlson, Richard. *Don't Sweat the Small Stuff for Teens: Simple Ways to Keep Your Cool in Stressful Times.* New York: Hyperion, 2000.

Lang, Denise. *But Everyone Else Looks So Sure of Themselves: A Guide to Surviving the Teen Years.* White Hall, Va.: Shoe Tree Publisher, 1991.

Desetta, Al. *The Courage To Be Yourself: True Stories by Teens About Cliques, Conflicts, and Overcoming Peer Pressure.* Minneapolis: Free Spirit Publishing, 2005.

Feller, Robyn M. *Everything You Need to Know About . . . Peer Pressure (Need to Know Library).* New York: Rosen Publishing Group, 1997.

Geddes, Melanie D. *Learning to Dream with Your Eyes Open: A Survival Guide for Inner City Youth.* Learning Series Press, 2005.

Juzwiak, Rich. *Frequently Asked Questions About Peer Pressure* Teen Life. New York: Rosen Publishing Group, 2008.

Kaplan, Leslie. *Coping with Peer Pressure.* New York: Rosen Publishing Group, 1999.

Koubek, Christine Wickert. *Friends, Cliques, and Peer Pressure: Be True To Yourself.* Teen Issues. Berkeley Heights, N.J.: Enslow Publishers, 2002.

Mccoy, Kathy, and Charles Wibbelsman. *Life Happens: A Teenager's Guide To Friends, Failure, Sexuality, Love, Rejection, Addiction, Peer Pressure, Families, Loss, Depression, Change, and Other Challenges of Living.* New York: Perigree Trade, 1996.

Medoff, Lisa. *SOS: Stressed Out Students' Guide to Handling Peer Pressure.* New York: Kaplan Publishing, 2008.

Meinking, Mary. *But All My Friends Smoke: Cigarettes and Peer Pressure.* Broomall, Pa.: Mason Crest Publishers, 2008.

Scott Sharon. *How to Say No and Keep Your Friends: Peer Pressure Reversal for Teens and Preteens.* Worcester, Mass.: HRD Press, 1997.

Slavens, Elaine, and Ben Shannon. *Peer Pressure: Deal with It Without Losing Your Cool.* Deal With It Series. Davidson, N.C.: Lorimer, 2004.

Weston, Carol. *For Teens Only: Quotes, Notes, & Advice You Can Use.* New York: HarperTrophy, 2003.

Stewart, Gail B. *Understanding Issues—Peer Pressure.* Farmington Hills, Mich.: Kid Haven Press, 2002.

Youth Communication. *Keeping It Real: Teens Write About Peer Pressure.* New York: Youth Communication, 2005.

INDEX

A

acquired immunodeficiency syndrome. *See* AIDS
Adderall. *See* stimulants, common names
AIDS 40
alcohol 22–24, 28
    data on teen usage 28
    dependence 22
    drunk driving 24
    effects 22–23
    and sexual activity 23–24. *See also* rape; sexual activity; sexually transmitted diseases
alcoholism. *See* alcohol dependence
America Online Instant Messenger. *See* cyberbullying, instant messaging
amphetamines. *See* stimulants
anxiety. *See* generalized anxiety disorder; obsessive-compulsive disorder; panic attacks; post-traumatic stress disorder; social phobia
appearance. *See* clothing; hygiene
ascorbic acid. *See* vitamin C
Asperger syndrome 131
athlete's foot. *See* hygiene
attitude 118–119
autism 131
autism spectrum disorders. *See* Asperger syndrome; autism

B

barbiturates. *See* central nervous system depressants
benzodiazepines. *See* central nervous system depressants
bias crime. *See* hate crimes
biological mental health treatments. *See* exercise, as a biological mental health treatment; medications
bullies 61, 129. *See also* bullying, solving the problem, helping bullies
bullying 4–5, 59–67, 129–131. *See also* cyberbullying; family bullying
    confronting bullies 75–76
        being direct 76
        eye contact 75–76
        posture 75
        practicing possible scenarios 76
    consequences 60
        mental effects 60
        physical symptoms 60
        school shootings 60
    definition 4–5, 59–60
    doing the right thing 129
    forms 62–65
        direct 63–64
        indirect 64–65
    solving the problem 129–131
        helping bullies 130. *See also* bullies; bully-victims; family bullying
        talking to victims 130–131. *See also* victims
        why teens are needed 129–130
    speaking with parents 78–79
        action plan 79
        parental interrupting 79

paying attention 79
   respect 79
   sitting down 79
   warning 78–79
speaking with teachers and school
   staff 76–78
   documentation 78
   no-tolerance policies 77
   written form of consequences
   77
steps to stopping it 65–68
   contacting schools 66–67
   involving the legal system 67
   seeking mental health help
   67
   speaking to school personnel
   66
   telling parents 66
   telling perpetrators to stop
   65
   tracking data 66
   understanding bullying 65
bully-victims 61, 129
bystanders 61–62, 129
   doing the right thing 129

C

calcium 111
cancer 40
   risk from genital warts 40
carbohydrate 108
   complex 108
   simple 108
caregivers 44
CD4 helper cell. *See* AIDS
central nervous system depressants 34
   addiction 34
   chronic use 34
   common names 34
   withdrawal 34
child support services 80. *See also*
   suicide, child protective services
chlamydia 40
   symptoms 40
   treatment 40

Chlamydia trachomatis. See chlamydia
cholesterol 107
   HDL 107
   LDL 107
civil law 126–127
   payment of money 127
clothing 118
cocaine 28, 32–33
   absorption 32
   addiction 32–33
   crack 32
   data on teen usage 28
   physical effects 33
   related neurotransmitter 32–33
codeine. *See* opioids, common names
cognitive awareness 70–71
   cognition 70
cognitive-behavioral therapy 90, 91–92
Columbine shooting. *See* bullying,
   consequences, school shootings;
   homicide
communication 70–75
   improvement techniques 71–73
     empathy 71
     listening 71
     respect 71
     thinking 71
     visualization 71–73
community agencies 134–136
   county agencies 136
   nonprofit counseling agencies
     134–136
   waiting list 136
criminal law 126–127. *See also*
   felony; hate crimes; incarceration;
   misdemeanor
crystal. *See* methamphetamine
cyberbullying 121–126. *See also*
   bullying; family bullying
   assuming someone else's identity
     123
   creating false identities 122–123
   definition 121–122
   instant messaging 122
   keeping track of 125–126
     instant messaging 126

social networking sites 126
text messages 125
other terms for 123
safety tips 123–125
blocking people 124–125
logins and passwords 124
privacy settings 124
report episodes 125
unknown "friends" 125
what to disclose 124
social networking sites 122
text messaging 122

D

date rape 41. *See also* rape
deep breathing 73–74
delta-9-tetrahydrocanabinol. *See* THC
depression 85–87
appetite and sleep 86
irritability, anger, and guilt 86–87
losing interest 87
poor concentration or agitation
87
suicidal thoughts 86. *See also*
suicide
time 86
Dexedrine. *See* stimulants, common
names
dietary fiber 108
dopamine. *See* cocaine, ecstasy,
methamphetamine: related
neurotransmitter(s); stimulants,
related neurotransmitters
drugs 26, 37
costs of 37
nonprescription. *See* alcohol;
cocaine; ecstasy; marijuana;
MDA; methamphetamine;
PMA; tobacco
nonprescription hallucinogens.
See LSD; mushrooms; PCP
data on teen usage 26
prescription. *See* central nervous
system depressants; opioids;
stimulants

E

EAP. *See* employee assistance
programs
eating 103–109
beverages 104
calories 103, 106
eating too quickly 105–109
hunger "sensor" delay 105
late-night 104
skipping breakfast 105
vegetables 104
ecstasy 26, 30–31
active ingredient 30–31
addictive behaviors 31
data on teen usage 26
mental effects 31
physical effects 31
related neurotransmitters 31
emergency safety plan 44
employee assistance programs 137
endorphins 92. *See also* exercise
ethics 15–16
evidence-based medicine 90
exercise 92, 110–116
as a biological mental health
treatment 92
at home 114
jump rope 114
weight lifting 114
yoga 114
education 112
find a partner 112–113
join a gym 113. *See also* YMCA
monitoring heart rate 115
morning vs. night 113
set realistic goals 113
with music 116
with television 114–116

F

Facebook. *See* cyberbullying, social
network sites
family bullying 79–80. *See also*
bullying, solving the problem,
helping bullies

family practitioner. *See* primary
  care doctors
fat. *See* monounsaturated fat;
  polyunsaturated fat; saturated fat;
  trans fat
felony 126
fentanyl. *See* opioids, common
  names
folate 111
friends 44, 47–51. *See also*
  friendships; sticky situations;
  management, reliable friendships
    academics 50
    athletics 51
    core values 48–50
      checklist 48
    drug use 51
    extracurricular activities 50
    maturing 49
friendships 51–57, 117. *See also*
  friends
    ending them 51–54
      cheating 53–54
      crime 53
      drug use 52–53
    making them 54–57, 117
      awareness 54
      joining school clubs 56
      part-time job 56–57
      practicing techniques 55
      shyness 54
      social phobia 54. *See also*
        social phobia
      taking community classes
        56
      teen centers 56
      volunteering 56

G

GAD. *See* generalized anxiety
  disorder
generalized anxiety disorder 87–88
genital warts 39–40
    appearance 39
    cancer risk 40

glass. *See* methamphetamine
glutamate. *See* PCP, related
  neurotransmitter
gonorrhea 40
    symptoms 40
    treatment 40

H

hallucinogen-induced persisting
  perceptual disorder 35. *See also*
  LSD
hate crimes 126, 127
hazing 7
herpes 38–39
    medication 39
    prevention 39
    symptoms 38
HIV 40–41
    immune system 41
    transmission 41
homicide 97, 131–132. *See also*
  bullying, consequences, school
  shootings
    emergency situations 131–132
HPV. *See* genital warts
HSV-1. *See* herpes
HSV-2. *See* herpes
Human immunodeficiency virus. *See*
  HIV
Human papilloma virus. *See* genital
  warts
hygiene 117–118

I

IMing. *See* cyberbullying, instant
  messaging
incarceration 126
indirect aggression 61
instant messaging. *See*
  cyberbullying, instant messaging;
  cyberbullying, keeping track of,
  instant messaging
interpersonal psychotherapy 90, 92
iron 111

L

legal issues. *See* civil law; criminal law
losing weight 109–110
    eat smaller meals 109
        five small meals 109
    enjoy "treats" in moderation 110
        eighty/twenty rule 110
    involve the family 110
    watch for "wasted" calories 110
        nutritional labeling 110. *See also* nutritional labels
LSD 35–36. *See also* hallucinogen-induced persisting perceptual disorder
    forms 35
    mental effects 35
    physical effects 35
lysergic acid diethylamide. *See* LSD

M

marijuana 26, 29–30
    active ingredient 30
    addiction 30
    data on teen usage 26
    health risks 30
    panic attacks from 30
marriage and family therapists 96, 135
    degree 135
    training 96, 135
MDA 31
MDMA. *See* ecstasy, active ingredient
Medicaid. *See* state-assisted health insurance
medical insurance 134
    mental health coverage 134
    substance abuse coverage 134
medications 92–95
    dosing 93–94
    length 94–95
    personality change myth 94
    pharmacotherapy 92
    reliability 93
    side effects 94
    three-month commitment 93

mental health risk factors 83–84
    environmental 84–85
        home 84
        peers 84
        school 84–85
    genetic 83
methamphetamine 28, 31–32
    chronic use 32
    data on teen usage 28
    health risks 32
    related neurotransmitter 32
methylenedioxyamphetamine. *See* MDA
methylphenidates. *See* stimulants
MH. *See* medical insurance, mental health coverage
misdemeanor 126
monounsaturated fat 107
morphine. *See* opioids, common names
mushrooms 36
    consumption 36
    health effects 36
MySpace. *See* cyberbullying, social network sites

N

Neisseria gonorrhoeae. *See* gonorrhea
niacin 111
nicotine. *See* tobacco, nicotine
nicotinic acid. *See* niacin
nonprofit agencies. *See* community agencies
norepinephrine. *See* ecstasy, related neurotransmitters; stimulants, related neurotransmitters
nutritional labels 106–109. *See also* losing weight, watching for "wasted" calories, nutritional labeling
    amount per serving 106
    percent daily value 106

O

obsessive-compulsive disorder 89
OCD. *See* obsessive-compulsive disorder

opioids 28, 33–34
    addiction 34
    common names 33
    data on teen usage 28
    physical effects 33
    withdrawal 34
OxyContin. *See* opioids, common
    names

P

panic attacks 88–89. *See also*
    marijuana, panic attacks from
paramethocyamphetamine. *See* PDA
parents 43–44. *See also* bullying,
    speaking with parents; bullying,
    steps to stopping it, telling parents
pastoral services 136
PCP 36–37
    addiction 36–37
    administration 36
    effects 36
    related neurotransmitter 36
pediatrician. *See* primary care doctors
peer pressure 2–9, 117
    definition 2
    emotional responses 7–9
    forms 3–4
        behavior 3–4
        comments 3
        material items 3
    risk factors for 5–7, 117
        being afraid of peers 7
        being friends with bullies 7
        changing schools 5
        lack of friends 5–6, 117
        lack of hobbies 6
        moving 5
        poor family support 6
        poor school performance 7
        poor self-esteem 5
    types 2–3
        direct 3
        indirect 3
        negative 3
        positive 2–3
Percocet. *See* opioids, common names

personality change myth. *See*
    medications, personality change
    myth
pervasive developmental disorders.
    See Asperger syndrome; autism
pharmacotherapy. *See* medications,
    pharmacotherapy
phencyclidine. *See* PCP
phosphorous 112
PMA 31
PMR. *See* progressive muscle
    relaxation
police 44
polyunsaturated fat 107
post-traumatic stress disorder 89.
    See also rape, consequences, post-
    traumatic stress disorder
primary care doctors 95–96
professionals. *See* marriage and
    family therapists; primary
    care doctors; psychiatrists;
    psychologists; school counselor;
    social workers
progressive muscle relaxation
    74–75
protein 109
psilocybin. *See* mushrooms
psychiatrists 95, 135
    degree 95, 135
    training 95, 135
psychologists 96, 135
    degree 96, 135
    training 96, 135
psychotherapeutic mental health
    treatments. *See* cognitive-
    behavioral therapy; interpersonal
    psychotherapy
PTSD. *See* post-traumatic stress
    disorder; rape, consequences,
    post-traumatic stress disorder
Pyridoxine. *See* vitamin B6

R

rape 41–42. *See also* date rape
    consequences 41

post-traumatic stress
disorder 41. *See also*
post-traumatic stress
disorder
relaxation training. *See* deep
breathing; progressive muscle
relaxation
retinol. *See* vitamin A
riboflavin 112
Ritalin. *See* stimulants, common
names

S

SA. *See* medical insurance,
substance abuse coverage
safe-ride program 44
saturated fat 106
school counselor 95. *See also*
school services
school services 134. *See also* school
counselor
guidance counselor 134
school district psychologists
134
self-defense 116–117
awareness of surroundings 116
serotonin. *See* ecstasy, related
neurotransmitters
sexual activity 37–38. *See also*
alcohol, sexual activity; rape;
sexually transmitted diseases
misconceptions about 38
sexually transmitted diseases.
See chlamydia; genital warts;
gonorrhea; herpes; HIV; syphilis
social mental health treatments
89–90
social networking sites. *See*
cyberbullying, keeping track
of, social networking sites;
cyberbullying, social network
sites
social phobia 88. *See also*
friendships, making them, social
phobia

social workers 96, 135
degree 135
training 96, 135
sodium 107
speed. *See* methamphetamine
state-assisted health insurance 136
status symbols 61
STDs. *See* sexually transmitted
diseases
sticky situations 11–20
contributing factors to 11
examples of 12–16
management 17–20
backup plans 18–19
consequences 19
decisions 19–20
experience 20
finding allies 18
honesty 19
identifying instigators 18
prevention 17
reliable friendships 17. *See
also* friends; friendships
remaining calm 18
stimulants 34–35
administration 34
common names 34
mental effects 34
physical effects 34–35
related neurotransmitters 34
sugars 108. *See also* carbohydrate,
simple
suicide 96–99, 131–132. *See also*
depression, suicidal thoughts
child protective services 97.
See also child support
services
emergency situations 98–99,
131–132
mental health response
team 98
outpatient treatment 98–99
psychiatric hospitals 98–99
short-term treatment 98–99
signs 98
stigma against 97

syphilis 39. *See also* tertiary syphilis
   phases 39
   symptoms 39

T

teen pregnancy 37–38
   emotional responses to 38
   rates of 38
tertiary syphilis 39. *See also* syphilis
text messaging. *See* cyberbullying,
  keeping track of, text messages;
  cyberbulling, text messaging
THC. *See* marijuana, active ingredient
thiamin 111
three, four-methylenedioxymeth-
  amphetamine. *See* MDMA
tobacco 25–29
   data on teen usage 26
   health risks 25
   history 25
   nicotine 25, 28
   quitting 25, 28
   withdrawal 28
tort law. *See* civil law
trans fat 106

U

uninvolved. *See* bystanders
university training programs 136–137
   research programs 137

V

vicious cycle of bad health 105
Vicodin. *See* opioids, common names
victims 61, 129. *See also* bullying,
  solving the problem, talking to
  victims
vitamin A 111
vitamin B1. *See* thiamin
vitamin B3. *See* niacin
vitamin B6 112
vitamin C 111

W

Windows Messenger. *See*
  cyberbullying, instant messaging

Y

YMCA 113. *See also* exercise, join a
  gym

Z

zinc 111